CHARLES
DARWIN

CHARLES
DARWIN

Arthur S. Gregor

*Illustrated with photographs
and drawings*

E. P. Dutton & Company, Inc.
New York

The author wishes to express his gratitude to Dr. Antony John Sutcliffe, Curator of Mammals of the British Museum, who guided him unerringly through the vast underground storerooms of the South Kensington Museum directly to the Darwin *Beagle* collection, and to Mr. A. Morris of the Inland Revenue Office who took time out of a busy day collecting England's taxes to take him on a tour of Charles Darwin's boyhood home in Shrewsbury.

The illustrations in this book are reproduced through the courtesy of the following: THE BETTMANN ARCHIVE: pages 40, 67, 80, 107, 112, 120, 128, 146. RADIO TIMES HULTON PICTURE LIBRARY, LONDON: pages 15, 18, 90, 153, 156. ROYAL NAVAL COLLEGE, GREENWICH, LONDON (HOSPITAL COLLECTION): page 37. CAMBRIDGE UNIVERSITY PRESS, publishers of *Diary of the Voyage of HMS Beagle* by Charles Darwin, edited by Nora Barlow: page 35.

Map on page 45 by Publishers Art, Inc.

For Diana and Toby Kurzband
with affection

Contents

List of Illustrations

Part I
Voyage

On December 27, 1831, the one-hundred-foot three-masted brig H.M.S. *Beagle* weighed anchor in Plymouth Harbor, England, and with a strong east wind blowing set sail for the Cape Verde Islands off the western coast of Africa. Commissioned by the British Navy to take soundings of ocean bottoms and map coastlines throughout the world, the little ship carried a crew of seventy-two, including seven officers, two surgeons, two servants, six boys, and three American Indians being returned to their home in Tierra del Fuego at the foot of South America. Among the members of the ship's company was a young man of twenty-two named Charles Darwin. His presence on the five-year voyage was to make it one of the great scientific adventures of all time.

1

Here's a boy, plays around with his gases and the rest of his rubbish and works at nothing useful.

DR. SAMUEL BUTLER,
HEADMASTER, SHREWSBURY GRAMMAR SCHOOL

"Shooting, Dogs, & Rat-catching"

Leaving the river road along the Severn, the boy dashed across the Welsh Bridge and up the street toward a large, imposing red-brick house that stood near the top of the hill. At full speed he ran past the gate and over a broad lawn, flung himself inside the front door, and rushed down the high-ceilinged hall into his father's study.

Gasping for breath he cried, "Look, sir! What is it? I've never seen one like this before." Clutched in his trembling hand was a large, black, curiously marked beetle.

Dr. Robert Darwin scowled down at his eleven-year-old son Charles, and said, "What are you doing out of school at this hour?"

"Please, sir, I believe I can get back before they lock the gates for the night. I wanted to see you and my sisters, and on the way I saw this new beetle, and—"

His father interrupted angrily: "You thought I'd be pleased to have you poking about the countryside for bugs instead of tending to your lessons. Well, I am not! According to Dr.

13

Butler all you do in school is patch together your classmates' homework and hand it in as your own. You've had three years of Latin and Greek, and I'll venture you cannot recite five lines."

Charles flushed deeply. He did crib his friends' homework, but then all the boys did that. And although he could memorize up to fifty lines of Virgil or Homer when he had to, they were completely forgotten within forty-eight hours. The truth was that he had no interest in what was taught in his school.

Shrewsbury Grammar School, in company with other well-known English secondary schools such as Eton, Rugby, and Harrow, concentrated almost exclusively on the classic languages. Mathematics, history, art, and music were neglected, and science was not taught at all. "We give 'em Latin and Greek," boasted Dr. Butler, the headmaster, "and when they have mastered that we give them more of the same." Accordingly, he divided his students into two groups: the clever ones, those who excelled in Latin and Greek and who received his special attention and favor; and the sinners and idlers, those who, like Charles Darwin, had no talent for languages, and toward whom he was cruel and despotic.

What especially annoyed Dr. Butler about Charles was that the boy not only neglected his studies but also wasted precious time with such outright nonsense as collecting birds' eggs, rocks, and coins, and performing chemistry experiments in the shed behind his house with his older brother Erasmus. What could be done with such a boy to make him see the error of his ways? In Dr. Butler's study was a dark closet called "The Black Hole" in which he sometimes locked boys up. On occasion he forgot his captives and kept them confined all night long. He also flogged his students, so often and

Charles Darwin, age six, and his younger sister Catherine. At the day school they both attended, prior to Charles' enrollment at Shrewsbury Grammar school, he was the slower pupil.

so fiercely that he acquired a special reputation for brutality among the citizens of Shrewsbury.

With Charles, Dr. Butler resorted neither to imprisonment in "The Black Hole" nor to flogging. He may have realized they would have no effect on the boy, or perhaps he did not relish a visit from the boy's father, the formidable Dr. Darwin. Instead he decided to shame the boy before the entire school. "Here's a boy," he announced in chapel, "plays around with his gases and the rest of his rubbish and works at nothing useful." The assembly rocked with laughter.

Charles Darwin never forgot the humiliation of that moment. Yet Dr. Butler did not consider himself a cruel man. Stern and pompous, he took his task of pounding the classics into the heads of his students with utter dedication. He frowned upon sports. Football, he announced, was only for butcher boys, and boating he forbade entirely, although the gentle Severn flowed just past the west wall of the school.

The boys were not to be pampered: skimmed milk and dried toast were quite enough for breakfast, and milk, bread, cheese, and water or small beer for supper. Any boy who obstinately persisted in feeling hungry after such feasts could always daydream about the pork pie that had appeared at table at Christmastime. Dr. Butler probably took it as a re-

Shrewsbury Grammar School, which Darwin attended from 1818 to 1825. As a schoolboy he was described as "dull and apathetic." Today his statue adorns the front of the building.

flection on himself when Charles's family sent the boy hampers of food on occasion. What was the headmaster to do if foolish parents insisted upon indulging their children with unnecessary luxuries?

Life was Spartan at Shrewsbury Grammar School. Charles slept, with twenty to thirty other boys, in a long, narrow room with a single window at one end. Since Dr. Butler considered bathing a luxury, there was not a single bath in the entire school for the students. Many years later, Charles vividly remembered the foul odor that used to greet him when he awoke on a damp winter morning. Although the dormitory was never heated, even in the coldest weather, Dr. Butler allowed each boy just one blanket. Once, when Charles returned to school after having been seriously ill with scarlet fever, Dr. Darwin requested an additional blanket for his son. The headmaster replied by suggesting that the boy had possibly been spoiled during his prolonged stay at home.

Charles led a sorry existence at school. Without anyone to turn to for encouragement, he considered himself a failure. The masters, quick to take their cue from Dr. Butler, marked him down as an ordinary boy who showed no promise of any kind. Charles, however, did have one comfort that made school life bearable. Unlike most of his classmates, who came from great distances, he lived close by. All he had to do was lift his head from his books, and he could easily see the familiar red-brick chimney pots and the tall trees rising from the Darwin lawn. A brisk run along the edge of the Severn and up the hill and he was home. . . .

From his tremendous height Dr. Darwin looked down at his son still clutching his beetle in his hand. Charles's father was more than six feet tall, and weighed well over three hun-

The Darwin home in Shrewsbury. Charles' father, Dr. Robert Darwin, conducted his successful medical practice from an office in his home.

dred pounds. Charles always said that he was the biggest man he ever encountered. "At your age," said Dr. Darwin deliberately, "it is high time you took yourself seriously. You care for nothing but shooting, dogs, and rat-catching, and you will be a disgrace to yourself and your family."

Charles lowered his eyes before his father's anger and slowly put the beetle back into his pocket. He had disappointed his father again. Why could he not be what his father wanted him to be? His father was a great man, admired and respected all the country round, sought out by everyone not only for his medical skill but also for his advice and counsel. Why could he not be worthy of such a father?

Leaving the house, Charles struggled to hold back the tears. The beetle had not counted for so much. He had just wanted a chance to talk to his father. He could not talk to his older sister Caroline, who was in charge of the household. He felt that every time he saw her she was about to blame him for something. His mother would have taken his side. But she had died six years ago. He tried to recall what she had looked like, but all he could bring to mind was her sewing table, her black velvet gown, and her deathbed. It was a short time after his mother's death that he was sent down to Dr. Butler's.

Charles resolved—as he had so often in the past—to be the very best scholar in school. He'd throw away his birds' eggs, coins, rocks, and even his prize insects. He'd give up his chemistry experiments. Fifty lines of Homer? He'd memorize two hundred and fifty! Oh, his father was going to be very proud of him. Never as long as he lived would he be a disgrace to his family.

He'd have to run if he was to get to school before the gates closed for the night. As he ran he prayed. If he prayed hard enough, God would keep the gates open for him as He had so often in the past. Running swiftly, he reached the summit of the old fortifications that surrounded the town and formed a kind of footpath. Suddenly he slipped and fell, landing in the soft earth seven or eight feet below. Except for a scraped knee he was not hurt. But what was this, industriously digging its way out of the soil? A small pinkish insect with black spots and a curved thorax projecting beyond the head. He pounced quickly, and the prize was his.

Again he began to run, forgetting his bruised leg, his father's warning, and his new resolve. Collecting was the greatest of all adventures, and in his hand he held the newest, choicest, and most precious beetle in all the world!

2

I do not believe that anyone could have shown more zeal for the most holy cause than I did for shooting birds. How well I remember killing my first snipe. My excitement was so great that I had much difficulty in reloading my gun.

CHARLES DARWIN

"The Man Who Walks with Henslow"

"You can't count that bird, Charles!" cried Captain Owen. "I fired the same time you did."

Charles was out bird-shooting with two of his friends, Captain Owen and Major Hill. At the age of sixteen he loved shooting as much as he had when he was a small boy. The first time he pointed his gun at a bird his hand had trembled so he could not find the trigger. At Maer, the estate of his uncle, Josiah Wedgwood, he'd place his shooting boots at the foot of his bed before he went to sleep in order not to lose a moment when he got up in the morning. Often he reached a distant part of the Maer lands before he was fully awake. He could tramp through the thick heath and the fir trees from dawn to dusk without tiring, forgetful of everything except the number of birds he brought down. To keep score he attached a long cord to the buttonhole of his jacket and tied a knot in it every time he brought down a bird. He had to be absolutely accurate.

Today, curiously, each time Charles fired, one of his companions insisted he too had shot at the same bird. Only when the day's shooting came to an end did they confess that they had conspired to have a little fun at his expense by claiming that they had fired at his targets.

They were more than a little surprised when he failed to see the joke, because they knew him as a good-natured and easygoing young man. They were unaware of the intensity of his passion for hunting. For him it was the only thing worth living for. It is true that on a few rare occasions he felt a bit ashamed of his complete absorption in the sport. At such times he tried to find excuses for it, persuading himself that finding game and managing dogs exercised his mind and trained his judgment.

But whatever of good value his mind and judgment acquired in the fields seemed to vanish when he got back to the classroom. He was as poor a student as ever. In disgust his father at last decided that keeping him on at Dr. Butler's was a waste of time, and the sooner he was started on his career, the better.

Dr. Darwin had no doubt what that career would be. In 1825, he abruptly removed his sixteen-year-old son from Shrewsbury Grammar School and entered him in the University of Edinburgh to study medicine. The headmaster must have heaved a sigh of profound relief at the departure not only of "dull and apathetic" pupil but also of an awesome and aggressive parent.

During the summer preceding Charles's entry into Edinburgh, Dr. Darwin sent him to call on his poor patients on the outskirts of Shrewsbury, hoping by this means to spur his interest in medicine. Faithfully following instructions, Charles methodically noted down each patient's symptoms and reported them back to his father at the end of the day.

Dr. Darwin then prescribed the treatment Charles was to administer on his next visit.

For once Dr. Darwin was encouraging. "You will make an excellent physician," he said. "I can already see that people trust you. Remember, you can give your patients nothing more important than confidence."

Charles could not imagine what patients saw in him to give them confidence. He suspected it was his father whom they trusted. They tolerated him only because he was the son of the famous Dr. Robert Darwin. Obediently he continued to make his rounds until the time came to go up to Edinburgh.

But at Edinburgh, Charles turned out to be as mediocre a student as he had been at Shrewsbury.

Charles blamed his teachers, and by all accounts they do seem to have been a bleak lot. The professor of pharmacy endlessly droned the same notes that his grandfather had delivered in the same hall fifty years earlier. The professor of anatomy taught his course by means of lectures because it was difficult to secure human bodies for dissection. And the instructor in geology was so dull that Charles vowed that never as long as he lived would he open a book on that subject again.

The cases he observed in the hospital clinic disturbed him, and the only two operations he attended, one of them on a small child, haunted him for years. General anesthetics were not yet in use, and patients under the knife were often fully conscious of their suffering. Charles could not bring himself to witness another operation.

Instruction at Edinburgh was undoubtedly primitive, but the truth of the matter was that Charles was not cut out to be a doctor, and it did not take him long to realize it. But how could he tell his father? How could he disappoint him again? Besides, it was not easy to talk to him.

Dr. Darwin demanded complete and immediate obedience from his children. It was his custom to deliver a full hour's lecture to his assembled family each day, and while he spoke no one dared move or utter a sound. Nothing could take place in the household without his express permission. If one of the children on a freezing winter day wanted a fire in his room, he must first secure his father's permission.

There was no sense, Charles must have decided, to an attempt to appeal to his father. Far better to remain silent and to avoid home as much as possible.

At Maer, twenty miles from Shrewsbury, lived Charles's favorite uncle, Josiah Wedgwood, the son of the famous founder of the Wedgwood pottery works. Reserved and ramrod stiff with others, Josiah Wedgwood had a very special feeling for Charles, and he treated him as though he were his own son. It was only natural that as soon as the school year was over at Edinburgh, Charles should hurry down to Maer, where he quickly forgot the gory operations, the sick people in the hospital, and the endless droning talk of his professors.

Summers were delightful at Maer. There were boating, riding, hunting, and partygoing. In the afternoon the entire Wedgwood family, including Charles's eight cousins, sat on the steps of the portico, "with the flower garden in front, and the steep wooded bank opposite the house reflected in the lake." Now and then a waterbird paddled into sight or a fish broke the surface of the still water. In the evening music and good conversation filled the air. And perhaps most pleasant of all was Charles's pretty young cousin Emma Wedgwood. Summers, however, had a way of ending, and then there was Edinburgh to be faced all over again.

As a relief from the boredom of his classes, Charles used to go to the seashore to collect marine animals. Sometimes he went trawling with the fishermen and brought back oysters, which he tried to dissect with the aid of a crude microscope. One day he wandered into a lecture given by the famous American naturalist James Audubon, who spoke on the birds of North America. Hours that he should have devoted to his studies he spent at the Edinburgh Museum, where the curator, noticing his intense interest in marine life, presented him with a number of rare shells to place in his collection. Natural science was beginning to absorb more and more of the young medical student's time.

One day when Charles was home in Shrewsbury, Mr. Cotton, a local citizen who made a hobby of geology, pointed out to him a large, oddly shaped rock, called the Bell Stone, that stood in the center of town. "Strange," the old man said solemnly, "nothing like it nearer than Cumberland or Scotland many miles from here. The world will come to an end before anyone can explain how this stone came to be where it now lies."

Mr. Cotton's words made a deep impression on Charles. The earth must hold other secrets just as fascinating. Geology could be far more exciting than the dull lectures at Edinburgh at which the professor had assured the class that "the apex of the mountain is the top and the base is at the bottom."

Dr. Darwin, however, took a very dim view of his son's interest in shell collecting, lectures on birds, and curiously shaped stones. The masters at Shrewsbury Grammar School were right: the boy was a failure, completely lacking in ambition or direction. His disappointment in Charles was compounded by the fact that his other son, Erasmus, whom he had also sent to Edinburgh, displayed no interest in medicine either, and was already embarked on an aimless life of genteel idleness. Charles was Dr. Darwin's last hope for a son who would count for something in the world.

Two years after Charles's admission to Edinburgh, Dr. Darwin sat down with him for a serious talk. As usual he did the talking and Charles the listening.

"What are you fit for, young man? I'll tell you: an idle sporting life. You fancy that because I have accumulated some wealth I am going to leave it to you so that you will never have to support yourself. Well, I do not intend to see that happen. If you do not much like the idea of medicine, then you are to be a clergyman. The Church is your destination."

Before we judge Dr. Darwin too harshly, we should remember that nineteenth-century parents were much more domineering than parents today. No one would have criticized Dr. Darwin had he insisted upon Charles's remaining at Edinburgh. Nor was there anything unusual in steering him into the Church. Upper-class sons with no particular bent or ambition frequently were diverted into the clergy, where they enjoyed a respectable, leisurely existence, and caused their parents no further trouble.

As far as Charles was concerned, the Church held as little attraction as medicine. But if his father wanted him to become a clergyman, a clergyman he would be, especially since he really did not know what he wanted for himself. Besides, there were compensations. If he became a country parson, he'd have plenty of time to pursue his hobbies, and mingle shooting with sermons and visits to the worthy poor with beetle collecting.

But before he could go into the ministry, he had to have a university degree. To enter Cambridge University he must pass a classics examination, and in the years since he had departed from Dr. Butler's he had forgotten not only all the lines of the Greek poetry he had ever memorized but even the letters of the Greek alphabet. He was therefore forced to sit down with a private tutor, and it was not until the beginning of 1828, in his nineteenth year, that he began his university career.

But it was the same story all over again. His studies meant little to him. The moment classes were over for the day, he went out to sing, drink, and play cards with a carefree lot of young men who were more absorbed in having a good time than in doing their academic work. With them he organized a society called the Glutton Club, which was devoted to trying out unusual dishes and playing "Twenty-one."

As passionate about hunting as ever, he could not wait to get out into the country, but practiced his marksmanship even in his rooms by firing blanks at a lighted candle. If his aim was accurate, the flame went out. The sound must have had a startling effect on passersby, for one of his professors once remarked, "Mr. Darwin seems to spend hours cracking a horsewhip in his room, for I often hear the crack when I pass under his windows."

Charles's delight in shooting, however, gradually diminished. One morning, going over ground he had hunted the day before, he came upon a bird that was not quite dead from the gunshot wound it had received twenty-four hours before. He began to lose some of his zest for a sport that brought pain to helpless creatures.

The passionate bird hunter now became an equally zealous beetle collector, able to recall the exact tree, post, or rock where he captured his prize specimens. One day, ripping the bark off a tree, he came upon two rare beetles, and seized one in each hand. The next moment he discovered a third, and in his excitement popped the one he held in his right hand into his mouth and then pounced on the newcomer. But before he could grab the prize, his prisoner ejected a bitter fluid, forcing him to spit it out and leaving him with just one beetle for all his effort.

His friends, caught up by his zest for collecting, were drafted into a beetle brigade. To his classmate John Herbert he gave the following orders: "Try to get these specimens for me: the violet-black beetle found under stones on Craig Storm and the bluish metallic beetle which is very common on hillsides. If you cross the ferry you will find a long smooth jet-black beetle under the stones on the waste land, also upon the marshy land near the ferry a small yellowish transparent beetle with two or four blackish marks on the back."

But John had neither his friend's power of observation nor his patience, and when he got back from his walks and proudly displayed his finds, Charles was apt to say, "Sorry, none of these will do."

John did not mind working for his classmate. Undaunted, he'd take up his gear again and go off on another expedition. None of Charles's friends minded. If this affectionate and amiable young man loved beetle hunting, then beetle hunting became their passion, too.

"Keep up your interest, and you'll end up in the Royal Society," someone said to Charles.

Charles Darwin, a member of the greatest organization of scientists in the world? Impossible! But one day he happened to pick up a catalogue of British insects that had just come off the press, and under the illustration of a rare beetle that he had discovered some time before he came upon the magic words:

"Captured by C. Darwin, Esq."

"No poet ever felt more delighted at seeing his first poem published than I," Charles later wrote. *"Captured* sounded so grand compared with *caught*. This seemed to me glory enough for any man." Perhaps the idea of the Royal Society was not so fantastic after all.

Charles's beetle collecting at Cambridge was largely unscientific, a continuation of his schoolboy hobby of gathering almost everything he could lay his hands on. He made no real attempt to classify his specimens or dissect them. But his interest in beetles led him to other fields, especially geology, and geology led him to John Stevens Henslow, a young man of thirty-two who was one of the most effective teachers at the university.

In the 1820's the sciences were not taken seriously at Cambridge. The classics, mathematics, and theology were the basic studies. Science was considered the pursuit of amateurs. It was taught by instructors who dabbled in far too many areas to know any of them well. The very word *scientist* had not yet come into common use. Henslow, however, not only took geology seriously but had very advanced ideas for his time on how it was to be presented. He took his students on field trips, and then asked them to his home to discuss their work.

Delighted with the enthusiasm of his new pupil, Henslow often invited Charles to accompany him into the countryside. They went out so frequently that Charles became known as "the man who walks with Henslow."

On one of their walks one day they came upon a mob dragging two men along the stony ground, their faces and heads covered with blood.

"Body snatchers! Body snatchers!" screamed the enraged mob.

Grave robbery was considered a particularly shocking crime in those days. Medical schools, barred by legal means from securing corpses for their anatomy classes, often engaged criminals to rob graveyards, and paid handsome fees for the gruesome plunder. To save themselves the trouble of breaking into closely guarded cemeteries, some of the less scrupulous body snatchers, it was said, practiced the fine art of murder.

It seemed to Charles and Henslow that the infuriated mob was on the verge of beating the two robbers to death. "Get the police!" Henslow shouted to Charles, and without thought to his own safety hurled himself on the crowd. So fierce was his single-handed onslaught that the mob drew back for a time, long enough for the police to appear and spirit the men off to jail. Charles never forgot the episode; recalling it many years later in his *Autobiography,* he said of Henslow, "I never saw a man who thought so little of himself or of his own concerns."

In April of 1831 Charles—to his father's great relief—at last received his university degree. He had become deeply absorbed in geology, and instead of rushing off to Maer as he usually did at the end of the school year he took a field trip to North Wales with one of his Cambridge teachers, Adam Sedgwick. Here, Charles thought, was the very man to ask about a scientific puzzle that had been on his mind for some time.

"Professor Sedgwick, a workman showed me a large tropical seashell he said he dug out of a gravel pit near Shrewsbury. Could you tell me, sir, how such a shell could have gotten to the center of England, thousands of miles from tropical seas?"

Professor Sedgwick smiled, "No mystery at all," he said. "Someone came along, tossed it into the pit."

But it was not at all that simple. Charles had seen many similar shells in the vicinity of Shrewsbury, so many that farmers used them to decorate their cottage chimneys.

"Suppose, Professor Sedgwick," Charles said slowly, "suppose no one tossed it in. Suppose it occurred there naturally."

"That," said Sedgwick, "would be a great misfortune for the science of geology, for it would overthrow all we know today about the rock formations of the inland counties of England."

Somehow, though Charles did not dare to say so, the answer did not satisfy him. Why wasn't Professor Sedgwick delighted with the find? A seashell embedded in the heartland of England. A tropical shell! And Professor Sedgwick was not even curious. All that disturbed him was that he might have to change some of his ideas.

And then what about the Bell Stone? * Two geologic mysteries within miles of each other. What a fascinating science geology could be if one did not reject, but rather welcomed, strange and troublesome facts! And just a few short years ago he had vowed never again to open a book on the subject.

Collecting and observing and then reasoning about his observations offered far more excitement than any other pursuit in the world. If he could make even the most humble contribution to natural science . . .

That summer Professor Sedgwick and Charles tramped the hills of North Wales, examining rock formations and searching for fossils. When Charles arrived home in Shrewsbury on the last day of August, right on time for the opening of the fall shooting season, he found a letter waiting for him that was destined to change the course of his entire life.

---

* Charles did not have to await the end of the world for the solution of the Bell Stone mystery. Within a few years he learned of the power of the vast glaciers that had once covered England to move boulders great distances.

3

The voyage of the Beagle *has been by far the most important event in my life.*

CHARLES DARWIN

"My Second Life Will Then Commence"

The letter was from Charles's friend and teacher John Stevens Henslow:

"I have been asked . . . to recommend a Naturalist as companion to Captain Fitzroy employed by Government to survey the southern extremity of America. I have stated that I consider you to be the best qualified person I know of who is likely to undertake such a situation. Particulars of salary I know nothing. The voyage is to last two years . . . In short I suppose there never was a finer chance for a man of zeal and spirit. Don't put on any modest doubts or fears about your disqualifications for I assure you that I think you are the very man they are in search of; so conceive yourself to be tapped on the shoulder by your affectionate friend, J. S. Henslow."

From other sources Charles learned that the ship was the H.M.S. *Beagle* bound on a voyage to survey the southern coast of South America, visit the South Sea islands and then return by way of the Indian Archipelago; that Captain Robert Fitzroy, aged twenty-six, had served as second in command on the *Beagle*'s previous journey around the world; and finally that the salary was to be zero.

The moment Charles received the letter, all thought of his country parsonage fled, and in its place there rose in his mind a vision of the strange places of which he had so often dreamed: the Canary Islands, Tierra del Fuego, Patagonia, the Falkland Islands, the Galápagos Archipelago, the South Seas, the Indian Ocean. What a chance to sail over phosphorescent seas and wander on tropical shores, gathering prize specimens and making new discoveries!

Desperately trying to hide his eagerness, Charles consulted his father. When his father seemed to hesitate, Charles said: "Please answer Yes or No. I promise that if you say No, I shall yield to your judgment and never mention the subject again. Do not think, sir, I am so bent on the voyage that I would go if it made you uncomfortable even for a single night."

"It's a mad, mad scheme," replied Dr. Darwin. "What's wrong with the ship that they've been unable to get anyone? Surely they've already offered the position to others.* I am telling you it's dangerous, unsafe, and downright uncomfortable. And when, may I ask, are you going to settle down? How would it look for a clergyman to go tramping around the globe? Or are you changing your profession again?"

But then he relented a bit. "Bring me one man of common sense who advises you to go and I will give my consent."

Charles felt his father was right. It was a mad scheme. Be-

---

* With his usual astuteness Dr. Darwin had hit upon the truth. The position had already been offered to several others, who had turned it down, among them Henslow himself.

sides, where in the world would he find a man who disagreed with his father?

The next morning Charles went down to Maer, where the entire household was soon buzzing with the story. Usually grave and restrained, Uncle Jos at once rose out of his seat and offered to drive Charles right back to Shrewsbury to have a talk with his father.

Josiah Wedgwood was barely inside the Darwin door before he began to demolish Dr. Darwin's arguments one by one. No doubt about it, the boy *must* accept.

Now, Dr. Darwin had always maintained that his brother-in-law was the most sensible man he had ever known. There was nothing he could do but graciously give way.

Charles had been very extravagant at college, and to console his father he said, "I'll have to be awfully clever to spend more than my allowance on board ship."

"They tell me you're clever enough," his father said wryly. There no longer seemed much sense in opposing his son's will. The boy could do no worse than he had already done.

Charles at once hastened down to London to meet Captain Fitzroy.

The commander of the *Beagle* was a dark, slight, very handsome, and extremely polite young man.

"On a vessel as small as the *Beagle*," he said, "we are going to be thrown into each other's company very frequently, and you must understand that things are going to be a bit cramped. We'll dine together, but I hope you'll not mind if on occasion I want the cabin for myself. Treat each other frankly and honestly, and we'll get along famously. If not, we'll wish each other to the devil. You must get yourself a case of good pistols, and never go ashore without them. We are set for a long voyage, but you are not bound to stay with us. If you are unhappy you are free to leave ship the first port we make. Don't make up your mind to come until you have had a chance to think it over."

Charles was very favorably impressed with Fitzroy. What he did not know was that Fitzroy had grave doubts about him. The captain was convinced that a man's character could be judged by the slant of his nose, and he doubted whether anyone with a nose like Charles's had the energy and determination needed for a long and strenuous voyage.

Within a few days, however, he evidently had second thoughts about Charles's nose, for on September 11th he invited him to visit the *Beagle* where she lay in Plymouth Harbor on the southwest coast of England. When Charles saw the ship for the first time, she was being almost completely rebuilt after her first voyage around the world.

"Everything is on a grand scale," Charles wrote to Henslow. "Mahogany is used throughout the ship and we have twenty-four chronometers aboard. We all think her the most beautiful vessel ever turned out in the dockyard. Even a landsman like myself must admire her. My chief task is to get on board and try to look as much like a sailor as I can."

The *Beagle* was a sturdy little brig of 235 tons, 90 feet long and 24 feet in the beam, carrying 6 guns. She was very deep-waisted; that is, her bulwarks were high in proportion to her size, and for that reason a heavy sea breaking over her could be extremely dangerous. Ships of this type were nicknamed "coffins" because so many of them had gone under. The *Beagle,* however, had already lived through five years in some of the stormiest regions on the globe without serious accident.

On October 24th, Charles moved down to Plymouth with all his belongings, ready to board the *Beagle* at the first opportunity. The captain of a ship berthed near the *Beagle*

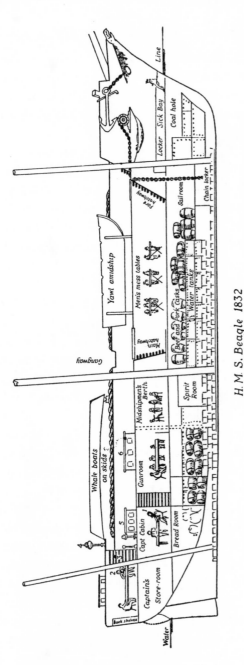

H. M. S. Beagle 1832

1 Mr. Darwin's seat in Captain's cabin   2 Mr Darwin's seat in Poop Cabin   3 Mr. Darwin's drawers in Poop Cabin
4 Azimuth Compass   5 Captain's skylight   6 Gunroom skylight

Side elevation of the H.M.S. *Beagle*. Darwin shared his tiny cabin with two of the officers. "I have just room to turn around and that is all."

solemnly assured him that in eight years of surveying the African coast he had buried thirty fine young officers. One day a sailor working on the deck of the *Beagle* fell overboard, and the body could not be recovered. It was an inauspicious beginning.

Swept by feelings of homesickness and the excitement of the preparations for the voyage, Charles suddenly developed a pain around his heart. Like any young student who ever opened a medical book, he was certain he had come down with heart disease. But fearful that he would be barred from the ship if his ailment was discovered, he refused to see a doctor.

Were his uncertainties the cause of his heart symptoms? All his life he had waited in the anteroom while others decided for him. Now, for the first time, he was deciding for himself. But to do so meant that he had to hurt his father as he had hurt him in the past. His exhilaration was probably tempered by a deep sense of guilt. His spirits, as he wrote to his sister Susan, ran one way and then another. Independence did not come easily to Charles Darwin.

The *Beagle*'s sailing was scheduled for November 4th, and Charles, forgetting all about his "heart condition," wrote: "What a glorious day the 4th of November will be to me, my second life will then commence and it will be as a birthday for the rest of my life."

The work of refitting the vessel, however, proceeded at a snail's pace, and the 4th of November came and went, and the *Beagle* remained in Plymouth Harbor. And now Charles wrote to Henslow: "We positively sail the last day of this month." But the last day of the month came, and still the *Beagle* did not lift anchor. "I look forward even to seasickness," he wrote again to Henslow, "anything better than this state of anxiety."

At last, on December 10th, the sails were hoisted, and the vessel rode out to sea. But a severe gale blew up, and the *Beagle* had to scurry back to harbor. On the twenty-first she

Captain Robert Fitzroy, commander of the H.M.S. *Beagle*. "Fitzroy's temper was a most unfortunate one. It was usually worst in the early morning and with his eagle eye he could generally detect something amiss about the ship and was then unsparing with his blame."

again put to sea, and again was driven back. Each time Charles became miserably seasick. He was never able to overcome his seasickness, and he suffered as much toward the close of the five-year voyage as he had at the beginning.

Charles was becoming better acquainted with his commander, and what he learned did not bode well. No two men bound together within the tight confines of a small vessel could have been less alike. Fitzroy was vain and arrogant, an aristocrat proud of his direct descent from Charles II. Fearful of a strain of insanity in his family, he was uncertain of his fitness to command, although he was a first-rate seaman. On one occasion he was overcome by a spell of black melancholy, retired to his cabin, and turned the ship over to his junior officers. A suspicious man, openly contemptuous of his crew, he was continuously on the watch for infractions of the rules. Even before the ship left England, Charles became aware of Fitzroy's varying moods.

Fitzroy could be overindulgent one day and savagely cruel the next. On Christmas Day, while the *Beagle* lay at anchor waiting for a favoring east wind, the captain freely dispensed liquor to the sailors, and the next morning chained and flogged them for drunkenness. Charles, lying sick in his hammock, heard through the cabin walls the thud of the lash against bare flesh and the outraged cries of the beaten men.

But the glorious, long-awaited day did finally come, and on December 27, 1831, the *Beagle* moved out to sea under a favoring wind, and held her course. The great adventure had begun.

4

The present is the child of the past.

CHARLES LYELL,
AUTHOR OF "PRINCIPLES OF GEOLOGY"

The Voyage of the *Beagle*

On January 16, 1832, three weeks after she had left England, the *Beagle* came to anchor at Porto Praya in the Cape Verde Islands off the coast of Senegal in western Africa.

Though only a few degrees of latitude separated Charles from home, he felt as though he were in another world. He stared with wonder at the high lava cliffs, the widespread coconut groves, and the stands of stunted acacia trees bent over at right angles so that, like weathervanes, they indicated the direction of the prevailing winds. He feasted on oranges at a shilling (or 14 American cents) a hundred, and listened to the native girls singing their wild songs and beating out the rhythms with their hands, their shawls cast on the ground about them. "It has been a glorious day for me," he wrote in his diary, "like giving a blind man eyes."

Fascinated by the behavior of a cuttlefish in a tidal pool, he watched it drag its body along with its arms and suckers

H.M.S. *Beagle* in the Straits of Magellan. "The voyage of the *Beagle* has been by far the most important part of my life and has determined my whole career."

and then suddenly dart tail first, with the speed of an arrow, into a narrow crevice, at the same time discoloring the water with a chestnut-brown ink. It seemed to know it was being observed, for it would advance a foot or two, almost like a cat playing with a mouse, and then speed away in a cloud of ink. As Charles, half submerged, poked about in the pool, the cuttlefish saluted him with a stream of water ejected from a tube on the underside of its body. He rewarded it for its good marksmanship by snatching it up and carrying it to his cabin aboard the *Beagle,* where it glowed phosphorescent in the dark. Charles doesn't tell us what his cabinmates thought of sharing their cramped quarters with a squid.

On the side of the cliff overlooking the harbor, Charles noticed a horizontal white band about forty-five feet above the water level. Examined at close range, it proved to be a thick deposit of seashells resting on ancient volcanic rock.

How could these countless shells have got so high above the water? Charles tried to picture what must have happened: A volcano had spewed forth lava, which, flowing into the sea, had hardened into rock. Later the rock had risen above the surface, carrying with it the soil and shells of the sea bottom. This island, like the rest of the earth, must have undergone great changes in the past.

But how?

Geologists were deeply divided in their thinking about how the earth had changed. The great majority, including Sedgwick and Henslow, believed in Catastrophism, the doctrine that held that the earth had been suddenly and dramatically changed by vast catastrophes such as the Biblical Flood. According to the Catastrophists, the earth was of rather recent origin. Some of them accepted the chronology of a bishop of the seventeenth century, the learned James Ussher, who had settled on 4004 B.C. as the date for the beginning of the world. Because they crowded past time into a small package, the Catastrophists were forced to assume that the changes the earth had undergone must have occurred with extraordinary violence and speed.

A small but growing group of younger geologists, however, believed in Uniformitarianism, the theory that whatever changes had taken place in the past had been gradual and uniform. The exceedingly slow and cumulative action of the forces that are acting on the earth at the present time, such as the wind, rain, movement of glaciers and rivers, earthquakes, and volcanic eruption, was held responsible for all past change also.

The Uniformitarians gave the earth plenty of time in which to change. According to them, not a few thousand years, but many millions of years were required for seas to rise and fall for islands to appear and disappear, and for mountains to climb out of the water and sink back in again. They maintained that geological history stretched far back into remote time.

The chief advocate of Uniformitarianism was the promising young geologist Charles Lyell, who insisted upon restricting his thinking to known and existing causes before he sought out extraordinary causes. He had expanded this theme in a book called *Principles of Geology,* with the subtitle "An Attempt to Explain the Former Changes in the Earth by References to Causes Now in Operation." *Principles of Geology* had a tremendous impact upon scientific thinking, and even Henslow had been impressed by the book. Before Charles left England he urged him to get a copy—with this warning, however: "Read it, yes, but don't believe it!"

Charles read the book, and he was just as much impressed with it as Henslow and the whole scientific world had been impressed. And as he looked out now at the white volcanic cliffside with its inlay of white shells, he may have imagined Henslow saying, "Quickly! Suddenly! Catastrophically!" and Lyell replying, "Slowly. Systematically. Uniformly."

Years of observation around the globe would go by before Charles was ready to make up his own mind.

Charles had his first sight of South America on February 29, 1832, when the *Beagle* dropped anchor at São Salvador (Bahía), Brazil. He could hear the noise of the insects in the tropical forest, although the ship was anchored several hundred yards offshore. Yet when he went wandering in the jungle a universal silence closed in upon him. There, in the lush rain forest, all his boyhood dreams seemed to come true. He was no longer an amateur idler sneaking off from his fam-

ly and teachers to indulge a childish passion. He was now
on a government mission, official naturalist to H.M.S. *Beagle*.
Almost overnight a boy's hobby had become a respected
adult occupation. All his life he had tried, and failed to satisfy the wishes of others. For the first time he was satisfying
his own.

In the months and years to come, Charles shipped back to
England crateloads of tropical plants, insects, flowers, spiders,
shells, and fossil animals. The crew, with whom he was very
popular, called him "The Flycatcher." To Lieutenant Wick-
ham, who was in charge of keeping the ship in tidy condition,
however, he was a nuisance. "If I were skipper," he said to
Charles, "I would soon have you and your damned mess out
of the place."

Except for getting his notes into shape, Charles did little
of his work aboard ship. He would jot down his first impressions in small, approximately two-by-five-inch leather-covered
pads that he took with him wherever he went. When he got
aboard ship he would write out a full account, checking off
his notes as he went along. These notes became the basis for
his book *The Voyage of H.M.S. 'Beagle,'* the story of his adventures during his trip around the world.

The ship was merely his means of getting from one scientific
task to another. As the ship slowly worked its way along the
Atlantic and then the Pacific shores of South America, often
retracing its route, Charles went off into the interior on expeditions of his own, picking up the boat at its next port of
call. On the five-year journey he probably spent more time
ashore than on the *Beagle*. When at sea, his principal occupation was, as he said, the "enjoyment" of seasickness.

"Nobody who has only been at sea for twenty-four hours,"
Charles wrote to his father, "has the right to say that sea-

sickness is even uncomfortable. The real misery only begins when you are so exhausted that a little exertion makes a feeling of faintness come on."

Among the prizes that Charles collected while he was in Brazil was a peculiar butterfly that could make a clicking noise loud enough to be heard twenty yards away, a noise that sounded like a "toothed wheel passing under a spring catch." Another was a small fish called Diodon that inflated itself into a ball and floated on its back in the water. If it were swallowed by a shark it could eat its way to freedom. "Who could imagine that a little soft fish," Charles noted in his journal, "could destroy the great and savage shark?"

Absorbed as he was in the profuse and vivid animal and plant life of the Brazilian jungle, Charles still found time to observe his fellow human beings. Brazil was a slave country, and what he saw horrified him. In the forest he came upon a former hideout of runaway slaves. Here they had cultivated a little ground and eked out a bare existence until they were recaptured by a company of soldiers. One old woman, however, rather than be led back to slavery, had thrown herself from the summit of a mountain.

One day he crossed a river with a slave who did not understand what he was saying. To make himself understood, Charles began speaking in a loud voice and gesturing with his hands. But the poor man thought Charles was angry and was about to strike him. Instantly, with a frightened look and half-shut eyes, he dropped his hands, a great, powerful man afraid even to ward off a blow.

Charles saw parents sold and separated forever from their children, a young Negro girl beaten and cursed by her owner, and a seven-year-old boy struck with a horsewhip because he had brought his master a glass of water that was not quite

The voyage of the *Beagle*. The *Beagle* took Darwin on a five-year, 4000-mile voyage to some of the most dangerous places on earth.

clean. Yet there were intelligent and even religious men, such as Captain Fitzroy, who actually approved of slavery.

Fitzroy, aware of Charles's hatred of slavery, insisted upon telling him about a visit he had made to a plantation. The master had called all his slaves together and ordered them to speak up and tell the stranger whether they wished to be free. "No," they shouted with one voice, professing great love for their master and recounting the wonderful treatment they received at his hand.

Charles could not restrain himself: "What would you expect them to say in the presence of the man who holds the power of life and death over them?"

Fitzroy was furious. "Since you do not credit my word," he cried, "we can no longer live together." He abruptly turned on his heel and walked off.

Charles took the captain at his word and promptly made arrangements to take his meals with the younger officers. But in his characteristic fashion Fitzroy soon had a change of heart, and within a few hours sent word to Charles that he was sorry.

In August of 1832 the *Beagle* arrived at Río Negro, the most southern settlement occupied by civilized man in South America. The country was dangerous because the Indians had recently rebelled against their brutal Spanish overlords. Yet Charles could not be deterred from exploring the region. Accompanied by a rancher who was returning to his estate in the north, a guide, and five gauchos, he set out across the waterless, treeless plains for Bahía Blanca, more than three hundred miles away.

He enjoyed the wild, independent existence of the gauchos and the experience of sharing their hardships and customs. "The deathlike stillness of the plain, the dogs keeping watch and the gypsy-like group of gauchos making their bed round the fire" made him feel millions of miles away from Shrewsbury. "I have become quite a gaucho," he wrote in one letter, "drink my Mattee and smoke my cigar and then lie down to sleep with the heavens for canopy as in a feather bed."

This middle-class young man, reared in a far gentler environment, was fascinated by these tall, dissolute-looking cowboys with their long black hair curling down the backs of their necks, their daggers stuck in their waists, and their great spurs clanking about their heels. "While making their graceful bow they seem quite as ready if occasion afforded to cut your throat," he wrote.

A great horseman himself, Charles was deeply impressed by the gauchos' skill and courage in the saddle. The thought of being thrown never seemed to have entered their heads. He witnessed a gaucho "breaking" a stubborn horse "which reared so high as to fall backward with great violence. The man judged the proper moment for slipping off, not an instant before or after the right time, and as soon as the horse got up he jumped on its back again."

In hunting, the gauchos used the bola, a missile consisting of two or three round stones covered with leather and held together with a thin plaited thong about eight feet long. Riding at full speed, the gaucho held the smallest stone in his hand and whirled the others round his head. Then, taking aim at his quarry, he hurled them through the air. Once an animal was hit, the balls wound about and completely secured it.

It all looked so easy Charles decided he must try. "Galloping and whirling the balls round my head, the free one by accident struck a bush and it immediately fell to the ground and like magic caught one hind leg of my horse. The other ball was jerked out of my hand and the horse fairly secured. . . . The gauchos roared with laughter. They had seen every sort of animal caught but never a man caught by himself."

Charles's toughness and stamina, however, won the unstinting admiration of the gauchos. He could endure hundreds of miles in the saddle over the roughest country, often getting up before dawn and riding many miles before breakfast. He could take extremes of heat and cold as well as any of them, and live on almost any kind of food.

Because of the Indian revolt the country was in a constant state of alarm, and all strangers were suspected of being spies. Fortunately, Charles carried a safe-conduct pass signed by General Rosas, the Spanish commander. As soon as the border guards saw the document, which began "El Naturalista Don Carlos," they were all respect and civility, although they probably had no idea of what "El Naturalista" meant.

Charles was shocked by the cruelty of the soldiers, who sabered to death every Indian, man or woman, they captured. The children alone were spared to be sold into slavery. Two Indians were taken alive to force them to inform against their comrades. They were placed against a wall with guns aimed at them, and questioned. But all the first would answer was "No se!" (I do not know) and the second, "Fire, I am a man; I can die."

"Who would believe," Charles wrote, "that such atrocities could be committed in this age in a civilized Christian country, and yet everyone is convinced that it is a just war because it is against barbarians."

The animals he encountered often seemed tamer than the human beings. One day he fired at a deer that seemed more startled by the ball cutting up the earth about it than by the report. When he got off his horse and slowly closed in on it, the animal in turn began to reconnoiter him.

Another creature that displayed no fear of man was the capybara, the world's largest rodent. Charles shot one that weighed ninety-eight pounds and measured three feet two inches. Among the many reptiles he collected, Trigonocephalus, a member of the viper family, was perhaps the most deadly. Gliding along the ground, it vibrated the end of its tail so vigorously that the sound could be heard six feet away. Charles must have gotten within even closer range, for he noticed that "the expression was hideous and fierce, the pupil of the eye consisting of a vertical slit in a mottled and coppery iris; the jaws were broad at the base and the nose terminated in a triangular projection. I do not think I ever saw anything more ugly, excepting some of the vampire bats." Then he added shrewdly, "I imagine its hideousness originates from the position of the features being somewhat like that of the human face."

Another creature that fascinated—and puzzled—Charles was Proteus, a partially blind reptile that lived in dark caverns. Why should its sight have been so poorly developed? The great French biologist Jean-Baptiste de Lamarck probably would have explained Proteus by saying that it had derived from an ancestor that had once lived above ground and had possessed the full use of its eyes. But once it began to live underground it no longer needed them and gradually went blind.

Lamarck believed in evolution, the theory that all life on earth had changed and evolved from earlier forms. Charles, on the other hand, went along with the overwhelming majority of the scientists of his day who were convinced that all animals and plants were much as they had been when they were created. Not until after his return home from the *Beagle* voyage did his views begin to change.

On the vast barren plains of the pampas, no matter where Charles looked, he found signs of life. Even the shallow salt lakes that dried up in the summer season and turned into beds of snow-white salt had their inhabitants. In the water he saw flamingos searching for the worms that lived on the salty bottom. What did these worms feed on? An even more primitive form of life. Here was a miniature world that somehow had become adjusted to living in brine. There was no region on earth, Charles concluded, to which life could not adapt itself, "whether lakes of salt, subterranean caverns, mineral springs, the wide expanse of the ocean, the atmosphere or the surface of perpetual snow."

The greatest surprise the pampas held for him was not the living but the dead, animals that had passed out of existence in the distant past and left only their bones to bleach on the flat red earth. He dug up many of these fossils himself. Others, such as the skull of Toxodon, an ungulate, or hoofed, mammal, a monster almost as large as a present-day elephant, he simply purchased from the natives. When Charles came upon the skull of Toxodon, it was lying on its side in a farmhouse yard. Two boys had been using it as a target for stone throwing when Charles rescued it. He paid a few pennies for what turned out to be one of his great paleontological treasures.

Among other prizes were Macrauchenia, an ungulate resembling a grotesque camel, and two ground sloths, Megatherium and Scelidotherium, so gigantic that they could rear up on their massive hind legs and feed on treetop foliage.

Perhaps the most startling of all of Charles's discoveries on the Patagonian pampas were not the remains of these great monsters but a single upper molar tooth of a horse that he found imbedded in a heap of fossil bones. A horse that lived at the same time as Toxodon and Megatherium could not be related to any of the horses he saw roaming the pampas. All these horses were the descendants of the European horses the Spanish had brought to America a few hundred years before. This tooth was as heavy as stone. That it was almost completely mineralized indicated that it had been in the soil for a very long time. This single tooth was evidence that long before the white man arrived in America a native horse had lived among Toxodon and Megatherium, and then, like them, had disappeared.*

The pampas were an incredibly rich mine of fossils, a vast, almost unending sepulcher of extinct gigantic quadrupeds. "If a straight line," Charles marveled, "were drawn through the pampas in any direction it would cut through an ancient bone or skeleton." At one time the whole area must have swarmed with these fantastic creatures.

It is difficult for us who reckon the age of the earth in millions and billions of years to realize what a tremendous impact these finds had on the young Darwin. Whatever others might contend, he could not believe that the world had begun a few thousand years before when he held in his own hands overwhelming proof of its vast antiquity.

Not only animals but also men offered evidence of the immensity of time. One day Charles came upon a massive arrowhead quite unlike those used by the Indians of the region. It was a relic of a long-vanished people who had dwelt on the pampas long before the present inhabitants.

He had barely absorbed the concept of the antiquity of life

---

* Today the tooth, together with the skull of Toxodon and other fossils Darwin brought back to England, is preserved in the Natural History Section of the British Museum in London. Unfortunately, a good part of the Darwin collection was lost when London was bombed by the Germans during the Second World War.

before another revolutionary idea came to him: these long-dead quadruped monsters seemed related to the living animals he encountered about him. The gigantic sloths out of the dim past resembled the living sloth. Fossil rodents were cousin to the living capybara. Extinct armadillos were built on the same plan as the armadillos he hunted and on which he so often dined. The Catastrophists insisted that great cataclysms had extinguished all life in the past. If that were the case, why should living animals be molded from the same basic form as those of the past? Was it possible that life had never been wiped out? Life began to seem not only long but continuous.

Charles gazed at the landscape, and the living animals departed. In their place Toxodon, Megatherium, Scelidotherium, Macrauchenia, the mastodon, and the native American horse rose and thronged the pampas. Then, as time rolled further back, these creatures vanished, and the sea came over the plain, and sharks and other ancient fish swam where he now stood. He was developing a long-range sense of time.

He began to see ties and relationships among animals living and dead where formerly he had seen only walls and distinctions. A phrase from Lyell's *Principles of Geology* must have often returned to him: "The present is the child of the past."

The young man who only a few short months before could hardly wait for the beginning of the hunting season now gave up shooting altogether, turning his gun over to his guide. "The pleasure of the first day's partridge hunt," he wrote, "can't be compared with finding a group of fossil bones which tell their story of former times with almost a living tongue."

Charles Darwin had put away childish things for a man's work.

5

I literally could hardly sleep at night for thinking over my day's work.

CHARLES DARWIN

The High Andes

At the beginning of March, 1833, the *Beagle* arrived at the lonely Falkland Islands in the South Atlantic. Treeless and barren, the islands were a desolate land of perpetual rain and snow.

In the midst of a raging hailstorm, Charles set off at once on a horseback tour of East Falkland Island, accompanied by two gaucho guides. Forced to cross an inland arm of the sea, they were often in water up to their horses' backs. Charles's horse fell at least a dozen times on the treacherous ground. When, after a two-day journey, they arrived back at their base, even the iron-framed gauchos admitted they were glad the trip was over.

In the Falklands, Charles came upon the only quadruped native to the islands, a wolflike fox so tame that it took food from a man's fingers. Though these beasts had overrun the islands in the past, they were now slowly disappearing. Some day they would be as extinct as the great mammals whose bones Charles had dug up on the pampas. Was it possible that what was happening to these foxes *at the present time* had occurred to other animals in the distant past? Had animals now extinct *slowly* died off, gradually diminishing in numbers until not one of them was left alive? Then no sudden catastrophe was needed to explain their disappearance. The very forces acting on life today must have acted on life in the past.

According to Captain Fitzroy, who took his Bible literally, animals had become extinct because Noah had refused them passage on the Ark. But Charles, who only a few years before might have considered such an explanation adequate, now sought, like Lyell, "known and existing causes" before resorting to "extraordinary agents."

Charles tried to work it out for himself: suppose a new species invades a region dominated by some native animal. The newcomer competes for the food on which the native lives. Should the stranger triumph, the native must eventually disappear. Competition among those that occupy the same place in nature (the same ecological niche, we'd say today) may then be an answer to the riddle of the extinction of species, the stronger always extirpating the weaker.

These random thoughts about the disappearing Falkland Island fox, though Charles could not have known it at the time, brought him close to the problem that would dominate the rest of his life: the nature of the process by which life evolves.

From the Falklands, Captain Fitzroy, bound on a strange personal mission, sailed for Tierra del Fuego, the great windswept island at the base of South America. He was taking back to their home three Indians whom he had "kidnapped" seven years earlier. On his previous expedition to Tierra del

Fuego, in 1826, one of his whaleboats had been stolen, and in reprisal for this affront to himself and to the British Navy, he had seized an innocent native family and taken them aboard the *Beagle* as hostages.

Having once tasted English food, the adults in the Indian family jumped overboard and swam ashore, leaving Fitzroy with three screaming infants and an eight-year-old girl. The captain rid himself of the babies by pressing them on some reluctant villagers but, oddly enough, retained the older child. Later, three young men (one of whom later died of smallpox) climbed aboard and insisted on staying as substitute captives.

Once he was back in England with his "hostages," the affronted captain became the benign patron. He gave his wards instruction in the elements of mechanics, gardening, and Christianity, and after they had been sufficiently "tamed" had them received by the King and Queen. But as the years went by, Fitzroy's conscience kept disturbing him, and he finally determined to get them back to their own people even if he had to charter a vessel at his own expense to do so. Fortunately for his purse, however, the Government decided to send the *Beagle* out again on another trip around the world, and offered him the command.

Accompanying the Indians on the return voyage was a missionary, the Reverend Richard Matthews, whom Fitzroy had enlisted to settle on Tierra del Fuego to look after the welfare of his three charges and convert their relatives to Christianity. Of the three Indians, Charles most fondly remembered Jemmy Button, who would come down to his cabin when he was seasick and murmur sympathetically over and over again, "Poor, poor fellow."

When Charles and a boat's crew from the *Beagle* landed on the southern shore of Tierra del Fuego, they promptly ran into a band of unfriendly Indians. The chief looked ready for the war path. His face was adorned with two bands of paint, one red and the other white, that reached from ear to ear and from the upper lip to the eyelids.

But once Charles had presented the Indians with some red cloth that they promptly flung about their necks, the chief relaxed and became quite cordial. To emphasize his friendly intentions, he ceremoniously bestowed three staggering blows across Charles's chest, then bared his own. Charles returned the compliment enthusiastically. Apparently highly pleased with his visitor's good manners, the chief then proposed a measuring contest. The Fuegians lined up back to back with the tallest members of the *Beagle* crew, and then, fearful they might lose, stood on tiptoe or edged up to higher ground.

The *Beagle* landed in Tierra del Fuego in December, the middle of the summer season in the Southern Hemisphere. Yet the weather was wretched; snow or sleet fell every day. It was a barren land heavy with mist or low clouds. The mountains were covered with perpetual snow, and great blue-tinted glaciers extended to the very edge of the sea.

Yet the natives did not seem to mind the cold. They were dressed in mantles of guanaco or otter skins carelessly thrown over the shoulder so that the wearer was more exposed than covered. One bitter day a woman nursing a newborn baby paddled out to the *Beagle* in a canoe. She remained alongside the ship for hours, probably out of sheer curiosity, while the sleet fell on her bosom and naked child.

Constantly in search of food, the Indians had no settled home, and lived on shellfish, seal, berries, or fungi. The floating carcass of a whale was a great feast. Their wigwams were temporary shelters made of broken branches stuck in the ground and covered with grass, rushes, or hide. They slept on the bare ground curled up like animals, barely sheltered from the everlasting cold and rain.

They must have originally come from warmer and more hospitable lands to the north. Why should they choose to remain on these miserable islands on the very edge of the continent?

They may have been wretched; yet, as Charles noted acutely, they were not dying off; their numbers were not decreasing. Somehow or other they had managed to make an adjustment to the climate and environment. Life, as he had already observed, had a unique way of adapting itself to the most difficult circumstances.

The Fuegian Indians may have been able to survive the terrible living conditions of the islands, but they were not able to hold out in later years against the European invaders. At the time of Darwin's visit there were almost twenty thousand Indians on the islands, divided into three tribes. Today, because of diseases introduced by white men and because of outright massacre, there are barely one hundred pure-bred Indians left on Tierra del Fuego. They may shortly become as extinct as the animals whose bones Darwin dug up on the Patagonian plains.

The *Beagle* was in constant danger during its stay in Tierra del Fuego, and yet Captain Fitzroy stubbornly refused to give up his search for the home country of his three "hostages." One day the ship ran into the most terrible storm of the entire five-year voyage. "The horizon," Charles wrote in his journal, "was limited by sheets of spray tossed by the gale. At noon a great sea broke over us and filled one of the whale-boats which had to be cut away instantly. The poor *Beagle* trembled at the shock and for a few minutes would not obey her helm; but soon like the good ship she was, she righted herself and came up to the wind again. Had another sea followed, our fate would have been decided forever."

On another occasion, when the ship's boats were drawn up on the beach, an overhanging glacier suddenly plunged into the water. A great wave rushed toward shore, and it seemed as though the boats were about to be dashed to pieces. Although in great danger of their lives, Charles and two other men ran down to the shore and made the boats secure. To commemorate the heroic deed, Captain Fitzroy named a nearby body of water Darwin Sound and a peak to the north Mount Darwin.

The "hostages" were finally landed and returned to their families, who did not, however, appear particularly keen about having them back. The Reverend Matthews was set on shore with a plentiful supply of provisions, food, and equipment, including such essentials for living in Tierra del Fuego as tea-trays, white linen, washbowls, pitchers, mahogany sideboards, wineglasses, beaver hats, soup tureens, and books. No sooner had Captain Fitzroy departed than word spread over the countryside that a rich stranger had arrived. The boats were hardly out of sight before hordes of men, women, and children came trooping down to examine the missionary and sample his fascinating wares. Instead of giving himself to spreading the word of God among the heathen, Mr. Matthews found that he had to devote his time night and day to protecting his property from them. Twelve days later, when the boats returned, he was forced to admit that his mission was a dismal failure. He rejoined the expedition and eventually settled in Australia.

It was just as well. Several years after his short-lived stay, other, braver, missionaries settled on Tierra del Fuego. In

1859, however, the Indians rose and killed them all. Ironically enough, the Indians were led by a son of Jemmy Button.

In July of 1834, two and a half years after having left England, the *Beagle* entered the Pacific Ocean and sailed up the western coast of South America to Valparaiso, the chief seaport of Chile, where Charles caught his first glimpse of the 23,000-foot high Aconcagua, the highest volcanic peak in the Western Hemisphere.

At last Charles was free of the bleak subarctic cold of Tierra del Fuego. "How different are your feelings," he exulted, "when viewing black mountains half-enveloped in clouds and then seeing another range through the light blue haze of a fine day."

But he had not come so far to enjoy the sunshine. At his very first opportunity he set out on an expedition into the Andes to do some "geologizing." On horseback, accompanied by a single guide, he swiftly climbed into the mountains, and on the first night camped twenty-six miles from Valparaiso. The air was so clear he could easily see the masts of a vessel riding at anchor in the harbor far below. The next morning he came upon shellfish fossils, and concluded that this vast mountain range must have risen out of the sea.

A few days later, standing alone on a peak with the Andes, the backbone of America, rising about him, he experienced a great sense of elation and pride. It was as though he were the first man who ever stood on a pinnacle and looked out on a view. As he gazed in wonder at the overwhelming mass about him, he realized that he could no longer believe in the old doctrine of Catastrophism. How could these mountains ever have been raised in one cataclysmic moment? Countless ages must have gone by before they achieved their sky-rending height. Lyell was right: nature could proceed only by gradual and orderly steps.

Within seven months of his arrival on the west coast of South America, the Andes presented Charles with a spectacular confirmation of his new views. On February 20, 1835, he was resting in a wood near Vladivia in Central Chile when suddenly the earth began to rock. When he stood up, he became dizzy and felt as though he were skating over ice that was buckling under his weight.

Although the earthquake lasted only two minutes, it was the worst in Chile's history. Innumerable small tremors followed the first great quake. Within the next twelve days three hundred were counted. Up and down the coast the earth opened, and great fissures appeared. In nearby towns and villages not a house was left standing. Bricks, tiles, and timbers lay scattered over the ground.

Shortly after the first shock, a great wave rose out of the sea and broke into a fearful line of breakers as it neared the shore. The first wave was followed by two others that deposited a vast quantity of wreckage on the beach and then carried it out to sea again. The whole coast was strewn with timbers as though a great fleet had been destroyed. Cattle were washed out to sea, and a four-ton cannon was carried fifteen feet inland.

But the most remarkable effect of the earthquake was *the raising of the land*. A few days after the earthquake, and thirty miles from its center, Captain Fitzroy found shellfish clinging to rocks that had been elevated several feet above high-water mark.

So that was the way land was raised! Land elevation and earthquakes were directly related. Each successive earthquake, going back many millions of years, had helped to create these magnificent mountains. No mysterious or unique cataclysm triggered by some supernatural power, but the very events Charles had just witnessed explained what had occurred in the past. The catastrophes of the Catastrophists turned out to be of minute size. No longer would he be surprised when he came upon shells embedded high on cliffs or mountain peaks. They were no miracle, but mute evidence that by slow degrees the land had risen out of the sea.

At the beginning of March, 1835, Charles set out to cross the Andes, accompanied by his faithful guide Mariano González and an *arriero,* or muleteer, in charge of a *madrina* and a pack of mules. A *madrina* (grandmother) was a very important member of any mountain-climbing expedition. She was a steady old mare who wore a little bell around her neck, and wherever she went the mules followed. The mule, an off-spring of a male donkey and a female horse, could carry on a level road a load of 416 pounds, and according to Charles possessed "more reason, memory, physical endurance, length of life and obstinacy than either of its parents."

When the travelers reached an elevation of 14,000 feet above sea level, they experienced air hunger, and had diffi-culty in breathing. Even the mules had to halt every fifty yards to rest. Charles felt a tightness across his head and chest as if "he had left a warm room and was running quickly in frosty weather."

The air was dry and crystal clear. Food dried quickly, and wood shrank. Because water boiled at a far lower tempera-ture than at sea level, potatoes left on the fire all night were still hard in the morning. When Charles rubbed his flannel coat in the dark, it glowed as though it had been washed with phosphorus. The hairs on the back of his dog crackled, and the leather straps of his saddle threw sparks.

From the top of the ridge that separates the waters flowing into the Pacific from those running into the Atlantic, Charles looked down on the Argentine pampas and watched the rivers "glitter in the rising sun like silver threads until lost in the great distance." Later, standing on the edge of a mountain torrent, he listened in awe as the current hurled rubble and rock into the valley far below him. These great mountains had risen out of the sea. Yet in time this stream, together with other forces of erosion, would wear them down. Mountain building and mountain leveling went on endlessly.

On this Andean excursion an event occurred that may have had a disastrous effect on Charles's life, yet he was completely unaware of the danger he was in.

Here is how he tells the story: "Near the town of Mendoza, on the Argentine side of the Andes I was attacked one night by the Benchuca, a species of Reduvius, the great black bug of the pampas. It is most disgusting to feel soft wingless insects, about an inch long, crawling over one's body. Before sucking they are quite thin but afterwards they become round and bloated with blood and in this state are easily crushed. One which I caught . . . was very empty. When you present a finger the bold insect immediately protrudes its sucker, charges and draws blood. No pain is caused by the wound. It is curious to watch its body during the act of sucking. In less than ten minutes it changes from being as flat as a wafer to a globular form. This one feast for which the Benchuca was indebted to one of the officers of the *Beagle* kept it fat during four whole months but after the first fortnight it was ready for another suck."

Neither Charles nor the officer would have been quite so ready to feed the insect with their own blood had they known what a dangerous creature they were handling. Only many years later was it discovered that the Benchuca carried Chagas' disease, an illness that can invalid a man for life. Today 70 percent of the population in the district where Charles was attacked carry in their blood the trypanosome that causes the disease. Once bitten, a man has very little chance of escaping infection.

On April 10th, after twenty-four days in the mountains, Charles was once more back in Santiago. "I have never made so successful a voyage," he wrote to his sister Susan. "I am sure my father would not regret it if he could know how deeply I have enjoyed it." Charles does not seem to have understood his father's real feelings. For Dr. Darwin, the whole *Beagle* adventure was a mistake from the beginning.

On his last South American expedition Charles undertook a five-hundred-mile horseback trip to Copiapó in northern Chile, where Captain Fitzroy had arranged to pick him up. He bought four mules and two horses for the journey, and later sold them almost for what he had paid for them. He was becoming a careful businessman. Dr. Darwin, who paid all his expenses, at least had no further cause to complain about his son's extravagances.

At first the road followed the coastline along the sea, but then it climbed steeply into the mountains. Snowdrifts covered the treacherous path, and the travelers were forced to dismount and lead their animals. At night piercing gales blew up, and the temperature dropped so low that a cup of water froze to ice.

While visiting the mines in the high mountains, Charles noted the way the Indian workers were treated. Starting before dawn, they worked until after dark for what would be the equivalent of fifty dollars a year. One gold mine was 450 feet below ground. To get to the surface the miners had to clamber up tree trunks, into which notches had been cut, while bearing on their backs a two-hundred-pound load of stone and rubble. If a lump of gold was stolen, its full value was taken from the pitifully low wages of the entire miner crew, thus forcing the men to spy on one another. The workers were fed bread and beans, but they tended to eat only bread because they disliked beans. When their master discovered they were losing strength, he forced the beans on them much as though they had been animals being fattened for the butcher.

Terrible as was the lot of the Chilean miners, that of the peasants was worse. In return for a small plot of ground, the peasant gave the landlord lifetime service, and never had enough time to work his own bit of soil. Only when his own children grew big enough to work could he rise above a starvation level.

The voyage of the *Beagle* took Charles to some of the most primitive places on the face of the earth. Yet he was never able to harden himself to cruelty and injustice. The terrible sights he witnessed as a young man remained with him for the rest of his life.

In late June, Charles reached Copiapó, where the *Beagle* awaited him and where he said good-by to Mariano González, with whom he had ridden so many miles through the Andes. The *Beagle* sailed north to Peru, and then, in September of 1835, left South America behind and turned northwestward into the vast Pacific.

6

You would be surprised to know how entirely the pleasure of arriving in a new place depends on letters. I saw the other day a vessel sail for England . . . how easily I could turn deserter.

CHARLES DARWIN

The Galápagos Islands

Captain Fitzroy's first anchorage in the Pacific was the Galápagos Archipelago, a cluster of ten volcanic islands just under the Equator and over five hundred miles due west of Ecuador in South America, with craters rising to a height of three thousand and four thousand feet. The *Beagle* had barely let down her anchor off Chatham Island, one of the principal islands of the group, before Charles was ashore exploring.

The island was studded with cones of lava. In some places the lava had spilled over the sides of the craters like pitch over the sides of a pot. Elsewhere it had blown into great bubbles that had hardened and then collapsed, leaving behind steep-sided circular pits. Out of cracks in the ground small jets of smoke curled into the hot, still air.

Clambering about the volcanic rock, Charles suddenly encountered two huge tortoises. "One was eating a piece of cactus and as I approached he stared at me and then slowly

65

lumbered off . . . The other gave a deep hiss and drew in its head." Amid the black lava, the leafless shrubs, and the cacti they looked like antediluvian monsters. On another island Darwin came upon the skull of the captain of a sealing vessel who had been murdered by his crew a few years earlier. The Galápagos seemed to be like the infernal regions, in good part sterile and arid.

These islands were not very old. Once, only the vast ocean had been here. Then undersea volcanoes had spewed forth lava from their vast underground fires, and produced these islands. Afterward life had come: low-lying shrubs, birds, insects, lizards, and tortoises, most of them species found nowhere else in the world.* Where had they come from? What was their origin?

For most people the answer was obvious: God had created them. If they were different from animals and plants found elsewhere, then God had made them for these islands alone. Not only ordinary people, but the majority of scientists, subscribed to the doctrine of special creation: God had brought into existence every species of animal and plant on the earth, and they had remained from the moment of creation just as he had fashioned them. Species were fixed or immutable, and could not change.

As a religious young man Charles may have preferred to believe that the Creator was directly responsible for the species he saw about him in the Galápagos as well as for all

---

* A species is a group of animals or plants possessing common characteristics. The individuals within a species resemble each other more closely than they resemble members of other species, and they are capable of breeding with each other.

Testing the speed of a tortoise, Darwin found that it could cover sixty yards in ten minutes. Observing that the tortoises of the Galápagos Islands belonged to different species, Darwin began to have doubts about the special creation of each species.

the others in the world. But the more closely he examined the forms of life on these desert volcanic islands, the more difficult it became to maintain his faith in special creation.

But if special creation was not the answer to the origin of these animals and plants, what was?

How could new forms of life have originated on these far-flung spots of land set in the midst of the broad ocean? What was the origin of these great tortoises that he encountered every day waddling in bands of hundreds toward the fresh-water springs in the interior of the island? Some were so huge that six to eight men could barely lift one off the ground.

These turtles craved water so much that they disregarded any human beings in sight to gulp down hundreds of great mouthfuls. For three or four days they stayed in the vicinity of the spring, replenishing their water supply, using their bladders, possibly, as reservoirs. Then, their thirst at last quenched, they padded back to the beach.

And what of the origin of the great black lizards that swarmed out of Charles's way on the rocks along the shore and then darted into their burrows? He watched a lizard gnawing at one end of a cactus while a finch pecked at the other end. Its meal completed, the little bird hopped on the back of the reptile. Some of the lizards climbed the low-lying branches of the acacia trees and browsed among the leaves. Lizard meat was a great delicacy among members of the *Beagle* crew, but after one trial Charles discovered it was only for those "whose stomachs soar above all prejudice."

Tortoises and lizards, lizards and tortoises: these volcanic rocks were overrun with reptiles. With the exception of a mouse, there was not a single native mammal on any of the islands. So must the world have been, thought Charles, during ancient times when lizards comparable in size to present-day whales swarmed over the face of the globe.

Even more surprising than the dominance of the reptiles was the fact that there were such a great number of them. More significantly several islands had their own particular kinds of tortoise. They differed in color, size, shape and, when cooked, even in taste. The birds, too, were divided into different species, some confined exclusively to one island. Charles counted thirteen different species among the finches alone. "I never dreamed that islands fifty or sixty miles apart, most of them in sight of each other, formed of precisely the same rocks, under the same climate, rising to nearly equal height would have been so differently tenanted!" To continue to accept the orthodox theory about the beginning of life, he would have to say that every last species of Galápagos tortoise, lizard, finch, and mouse was the result of an individual act of creation. Incredible that the Creator should have busied Himself turning out new and different species for some of these desert islands.

Yet another observation: here he was on a lonely Pacific island more than five hundred miles from America, and yet the animal and plant life he saw about him constantly reminded him of that continent. He was surrounded "by new birds, new reptiles, new shells, new insects, new plants and yet by innumerable trifling details, such as the tone of voices and the plumage of the birds, they bring to mind the plains of Patagonia and the hot dry deserts of Northern Chile." Why was life on these small points of land so closely related to what he had left behind in South America? If these Galápagos species were specially created, should they not be quite different from those on the mainland?

Well, suppose you do cast some doubt on the idea of special creation in which science, religion, your teachers, your friends, and your family firmly believe. Can you, Charles Darwin, walking on this hot sultry day over the rough volcanic rocks of Chatham Island, offer anything in its place? Can you free yourself of all prejudice and examine these questions as though you were the first man in the world ever to confront them? Why should the species of the Galápagos bear a relation to those of the continent? Why should some of these islands have their own particular species of plant or animal?

Whether you wish it or no, you have just two choices: either new species were specially created for the Galápagos or species migrated from South America and in some manner took on new characteristics after their arrival. In other words they changed from one species to another.

You don't know the answer. All you know is that you can no longer take the usual answers for granted. The question will arise again and again; pursue you to England and not allow you to rest until you decide to make the solution your lifework.*

Toward the end of October, 1835, Captain Fitzroy completed his survey of the Galápagos Islands. Charles loaded his store of specimens aboard ship, and the *Beagle* set out across the broad Pacific once more. After brief stops in Tahiti, where Charles discovered that it did not take long "to make a dark skin more attractive and natural to the eye of a European than his own," and then New Zealand, the ship reached Australia in January of 1836. He had now spent five Christmases away from home, and he longed for his family and England.

Charles went kangaroo hunting, but all he was able to catch was a kangaroo rat. The country had formerly abounded in native animals, but now both the kangaroo and the emu

---

* Up to this point in his career, Darwin had thought of himself as primarily a geologist. Although he never abandoned his interest in geology, what he saw in the Galápagos helped to anchor his attention to the life sciences.

were disappearing. Charles was lucky to come upon a single duck-billed platypus, the extraordinary Australian mammal that lays eggs. The native animals were being killed off by the dogs of the white settlers.

The aboriginal population was also steadily declining. A mild European illness such as measles became a deadly plague among people who had never been exposed to it before. "Wherever the European has trod," Charles wrote, "death seems to pursue the aboriginal." In New Zealand he had heard the native Maori lament that they were doomed in the struggle for existence. A Maori saying went: "As the white man's rat has driven away the native rat, so the European fly has driven away our fly, so the clover kills our fern, and so will the Maori himself disappear before the white man." And the story was the same in America, Polynesia, the Cape of Good Hope, Australia: men seemed to act on each other as though they were competing species of animals. Let invader and native come face to face, and a struggle for existence followed in which the native was crushed and eventually disappeared.

From Australia the *Beagle* set sail for the Keeling, or Cocos, Islands in the Indian Ocean six hundred miles south of Sumatra. These islands were made of coral, tiny living animals whose lime skeletons had built up the land in the midst of the sea. These low, insignificant coral islets outlasted islands made of the hardest granite. "The accumulated labor of myriads of architects at work night and day, month after month" eventually conquered "the great mechanical power of the waves of the ocean." *

---

* Many years later, in his last scientific investigation (see page 158), Charles was similarly impressed with the cumulative efforts of another small creature, the earthworm. Like the coral, the earthworm, over vast periods of time, brings about profound geological changes.

In the Keeling Islands Charles found a crab that lived on coconuts. The crab was able to tear off the husk, fiber by fiber, and then with its very heavy and unusual claws keep hammering until it cracked open the shell of a coconut. Crabs and coconuts: what could be more remote? Charles wondered. Yet nature had furnished this animal with a peculiar adaptation of its claws by which the gap could be bridged.

In July, 1836, the *Beagle* reached tiny Ascension Island in the South Atlantic, where a letter from Adam Sedgwick awaited Charles. His collection and notes had arrived in England, and they were creating quite a stir in scientific circles. Sedgwick had called on Dr. Darwin and predicted a distinguished scientific career for his son. Charles could not restrain himself: "After reading this letter I clambered over the mountains with a bounding step and made the volcanic rocks resound under my geological hammer."

Gone forever was the danger that he would disgrace himself and his family. He was becoming the man his father wanted him to be, good for something better than "shooting, dogs, and rat-catching."

Charles would have been even more elated had he seen a letter that Sedgwick had written to Dr. Butler, Charles's old headmaster at Shrewsbury Grammar School:

"It was the best thing in the world for him that he went on the voyage. There was some danger of his turning into an idle man . . . but if God spares his life he will have a great name among the naturalists of Europe."

The *Beagle* had now completed a circuit of the entire globe, and Charles was becoming more and more impatient to be home. "I doubt whether ever boy longed for his holidays," he write to his family, "as much as I do to see you all again."

But to the dismay of the entire ship's company, Captain Fitzroy gave the command: *West-southwest!* The *Beagle* was not yet ready to go home.

Overcome by one of his periodic bouts of conscience, Captain Fitzroy was returning to South America. Had he really completed his chronological survey? What had he omitted? Best to go back and double-check his results. So once more the *Beagle* crossed the Atlantic, reaching Bahía in Brazil in August of 1836. Again Charles walked through the tropical jungle, absorbing the forms of the mango, palm, fern, coconut and banana trees as though he hoped to preserve forever the memory of that "great wild untidy luxuriant hothouse." Yet he was also glad to see the last of Brazil, for that country would always remain for him a land of cruelty, suffering, and inhumanity.

At last the *Beagle* sailed for home. As England came nearer, and he realized that the journey was finally coming to a close, Charles tried to summon up the highlights of his five-year trip around the globe.

He remembered the look of the sea one night as the ship sailed south of the Río de la Plata off the coast of Argentina: "There was a fresh breeze and every part of the surface which during the day is seen as foam now glowed with a pale light. The vessel drove before her bows two billows of liquid phosphorus and in her wake she was followed by a milky train."

He recalled "the Southern Cross, the cloud of Magellan and the other constellations of the Southern Hemisphere, the water spout, the glacier overhanging the sea in a bold precipice, a lagoon island raised by coral, an active volcano and a violent earthquake. For everyone an earthquake must be a most impressive event: the solid earth oscillates beneath our feet and seeing the labored works of man in a moment over-thrown we feel the insignificance of his boasted power."

But what left an even deeper impression on him was "the primeval forests undefaced by the hand of man whether those of Brazil where life predominates or those of Tierra del Fuego where Death and Decay prevail. No one can stand in these solitudes unmoved and not feel there is more in man than the mere breath of his body."

After a voyage about the globe, the world was no longer a blank sphere, but "a picture full of the most varied and animated figures. Islands no longer are mere specks on a map but assume their true size often larger than the kingdoms of Europe. Only when sailing for weeks along small portions of their shores are you convinced of the vast spaces of our immense world."

Would he recommend such a journey to a young naturalist? He certainly would. Let him be assured "he will meet with no difficulties or dangers, nearly as bad as those he anticipates. It will teach him good-humored patience, freedom from selfishness, and the habit of acting for himself. He will also discover how many truly kind-hearted people there are with whom he never before had, or ever again will have any further communication, who yet are ready to offer him the most disinterested assistance." But one word of caution: "If a person suffer much from sea sickness let him weigh it heavily in the balance" before he undertakes such a voyage. "It is no trifling evil, cured in a week."

Charles spoke from sad experience.

Charles had left England an amateur beetle hunter and sportsman, an aimless drifter from one profession to another. He returned a dedicated naturalist with a collection that brought him fame and made him a pioneer in the study of the paleontology of South America. The remains of Toxodon, Megatherium, Glyptodon (the fossil armadillo with the spiked tail), and the native American horse were carefully studied and admired by England's leading scientists.

So great was Darwin's reputation after his return that when Joseph Hooker, who later became his best friend, applied for appointment as naturalist aboard H.M.S. *Erebus* bound on an Antarctic expedition, he was told that he could not be considered because "a naturalist must be well acquainted with every branch of natural history and must be well-known to the world, such a person as Mr. Darwin!" Hooker indignantly replied, "What was Mr. Darwin before he went out on the *Beagle*?" Hooker got the job.

Charles modestly said that he returned "a millionaire in odd and curious facts." But he had actually uncovered something far more important on his journey than a storehouse of facts.

He had departed a pupil of Henslow and Sedgwick, convinced that the history of the earth was short and that whatever changes had occurred were the result of vast catastrophes. He returned a disciple of Lyell, converted to the view that the earth was extremely ancient and that its growth was the cumulative result of innumerable small changes.

In England scientists had had little opportunity to see dramatic geological change. Earthquakes were thought of as events in the distant past having little influence on what was happening in the present. But Charles had actually witnessed beaches being suddenly wrenched above their former level. He had seen evidence of mountain building and mountain erosion. He had studied the microscopic animals that had, speck by speck, constructed the great coral islands of the

Indian and Pacific oceans with the lime of their own bodies His own eyes told him that geologic change was as much a part of the present as it was of the past.

Before the voyage of the *Beagle* he might have been content to explain natural events by reference to the Bible or to a supernatural agency. Such explanations no longer satisfied him. Now he sought for the cause of things within nature itself. He insisted upon applying to the natural sciences— geology, botany, and zoology—the objective approach of the mathematical sciences—chemistry, and physics.

The voyage of the *Beagle* was the most significant event in the life of Charles Darwin. It made him a tough-minded modern scientist.

Part II

Discovery

Out of Charles Darwin's five-year adventure aboard H.M.S. *Beagle* emerged a discovery that shook the nineteenth-century world to its foundations and eventually revolutionized man's way of thinking about both life itself and his own place in the scheme of things.

Just when Darwin sought to express the first formulation of his discovery, he fell victim to a mysterious malady that made him an invalid for the rest of his life. The stalwart young man who had climbed the icy peaks of the Andes and outridden his guides over plain and desert was now imprisoned within the confines of his own house.

Yet, despite his lack of freedom and his intense suffering, he patiently and laboriously brought together the monumental evidence for the scientific explanation of the evolution of life: the principle of natural selection.

7

Animals, our brothers in disease, death and suffering, our slaves in the most laborious work, our companions in amusement, may partake of our origin in one common ancestor.

CHARLES DARWIN

"Like Confessing a Murder"

On October 2, 1836, five years almost to the day after Charles had left home, the *Beagle* arrived in Falmouth Harbor. The gangplank was barely down before Charles was ashore and on the stagecoach bound for Shrewsbury.

He had left home in many ways younger than his twenty-two years. He returned fully a man. Father and son sized each other up, and the father gave way. Despite his faults, Dr. Darwin was a keen judge of character. "Why the shape of his head is quite altered," he joked. He knew he could no longer treat his son as a child. There was no longer the slightest question about Charles's career. Not medicine, not the Church, but science, and Dr. Darwin had no choice but to go along with his son's decision. The voyage of the *Beagle* marked Charles Darwin's initiation into manhood.

After a brief visit to Maer, Charles went to Cambridge, where he spent the winter working on his *Beagle* collection

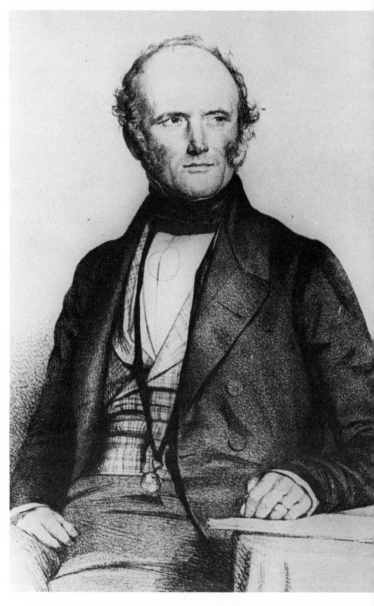

Charles Lyell, whose book, *Principles of Geology,* started Darwin on the road to his grand design.

nd getting the journal of his experiences ready for publica-
ion. In the spring he moved down to London and set up his
wn lodgings on Great Marlborough Street in the heart of
own just off Piccadilly Circus.

He was elected secretary of the Geological Society and
net Charles Lyell and other leading scientists and writers,
ncluding the famous author Thomas Carlyle, a good friend
of his older brother Erasmus. He remembered one dinner
at which Carlyle held forth all evening on the value of silence.
Some of Carlyle's opinions, his opposition to science, and
especially his defense of slavery aroused Charles's anger, yet
he never spoke up in his presence.

The bold adventurer who had freely exposed himself to
great privation and danger on his journey around the world
shrank from getting into a dispute. All his life Charles Darwin
led from public argument, and yet, single-handedly, he pro-
voked the greatest controversy of the nineteenth century by
championing the revolutionary doctrine of evolution.

From the day he landed in England, the questions that had
arisen in his mind about the origin of plants and animals kept
troubling him. By July of 1837 he had completely reversed
his previous faith in the fixity of species and had become convinced that the basic law of life is not unchangeability but
evolution.

He was not the first to whom the idea of evolution occurred.
In ancient times the Greeks had speculated about it, and in
the first century B.C. the Roman poet Lucretius had gone so
far as to say that man's origin was not godlike but animal.
Later, in the Middle Ages, however, men accepted the Biblical
story that the world and all its creatures had been brought
forth by God and the book of creation closed. All living things
therefore remained in just about the state they were at the

beginning. Evolution required vast ages for change to take place, but according to the orthodox the world was very young. In the seventeenth century James Ussher, Archbishop of Armagh in Ireland, by totaling the number of generations recorded in the Bible since Adam and Eve had come to the conclusion that the world was only six thousand years old. By refining his methods some of his colleagues had pinpointed the very moment of creation: October 23, 4004 B.C., at nine o'clock in the morning.

The archbishop's chronology came under severe attack in the eighteenth century when the geologists James Hutton and William Smith offered evidence that the earth was not thousands but millions of years old. Given a world of vast antiquity, the argument of the evolutionists could begin to make sense.

The first consistent champion of evolution in modern times was a member of Charles's family, his grandfather Erasmus Darwin. In 1794, in a book called *Zoonomia,* he suggested that millions of years before the appearance of man on earth all warm-blooded creatures could have arisen from "one living filament" and that the ancestors of man had been aquatic creatures that eventually made their way to dry land and became air-breathing.

Known as the English Benjamin Franklin, Erasmus Darwin was one of the most versatile men of his time. He was a poet, inventor, and physician with a medical reputation so great that King George III offered him the position of court doctor. He was a witty conversationalist with a wide circle of friends, including James Watt, Joseph Priestley, and the French philosopher Jean-Jacques Rousseau.

Extremely popular, especially with the ladies, he was no beauty. His face was badly marred by smallpox scars, and he was so stout that a semicircular hole had to be cut into his dining-room table to accommodate his enormous girth. His son Robert, Charles's father, may have inherited a disposition toward obesity from him.

As a boy Charles had dutifully tried to read his grandfather's book on evolution but could make nothing of it. In later life he was to say that though it contained many ideas, they were supported by few facts. Charles's enormous contribution to the development of evolutionary theory owes little or nothing to the views of his extraordinary grandfather.

The most distinguished advocate of evolution before Darwin was the Chevalier de Lamarck, the French student of zoology. He saw no need for universal catastrophes, but imagined that nature acted by slow degrees instead. Man arising from the primates was the "final result of the gradual development and improvement of all of nature's creatures." *

But in 1837, when Charles set down his first secret thoughts about evolution, he was almost alone. No scientist had taken his grandfather seriously, and Lamarck had had little influence on his own generation. The state, the clergy, the professors, the press, and the scientists would all have been shocked had they known what the promising young naturalist on Great Marlborough Street had in mind. "A fool!" they would have cried. "Worse, a heretic!"

Out of Darwin's experiences in the jungles of Brazil, on the pampas of the Argentine, in the mountains of Chile, and on the islands of the Pacific grew the overwhelming conviction that species had not been separately created but had gradually

---

* Although Lamarck is one of the towering figures in the development of modern biological science, his reputation today is overshadowed by that of Darwin. It is unfortunate that we remember him today not for his positive contributions but for one of his errors: the concept of the inheritance of acquired characteristics.

evolved out of lower forms. Once this concept became part of him, all his observations on his world journey began to make sense. The pieces of the jigsaw began to fall into place.

It was no mere matter of chance that the great extinct monsters and the living animals of the pampas resembled each other. They were related to each other through a common ancestor. The varied types of finch that inhabited the different islands of the Galápagos were similar to those of South America because they were descended from birds of that continent. They differed slightly from island to island because each species was adapted to a slightly different way of life: one, for example, fed on tree insects, and another picked seeds from the ground. The stamp of America lay upon most of the animals and plants he had seen about him in the Galápagos.

Now he understood how the plants and animals of these far-flung islands could remind him of "the plains of Patagonia and the hot dry deserts of Northern Chile." The birds, reptiles, insects, and plants of the Galápagos had evolved from ancestors that had come over from the continent.

Each living species, then, was not specially created but had evolved out of earlier forms. The explanation of nature's variety was to be found within nature itself. The mountains of the earth were not the result of specific acts on the part of God, nor were the living things that inhabited the earth. Lyell's principle of orderly uniform change applied not only to the formation of the planet but also to the development of life.

And what of man? Was man to be included in the evolutionary plan along with the beasts and the plants? Darwin did not shrink from the inescapable conclusion: "Man thinks himself a great work worthy of creation by the deity. It would be more humble on his part to consider himself created from animals . . . animals, our brothers in disease, death, and suffering, our slaves in the most laborious work, our companions in amusement, may partake of our origin in one common ancestor. We may be all melted together."

Once Darwin had jotted down these first thoughts, the world would never again be the same. The sweeping theory to which "the millionaire in odd and curious facts" determined to devote his life ultimately demolished many of the most comforting ideas of the past and brought about a revolution that forever altered Western man's relation to the Deity and to his own place in the scheme of things.

Darwin fully appreciated the price he might have to pay. The fate of early martyrs to science who had undergone imprisonment and even death for their cause rose in his mind. Yet he was determined to go ahead no matter how much he suffered. "And though I shall get more kicks than half-pennies, I will, life serving, attempt my work." And then he nobly added: "Those who believe and yet do not openly avow their belief as much retard the progress of science as those whose false opinions they assail."

Curiously, he began to suffer—in an altogether unexpected way—long before any other man heard of or even suspected his secret thoughts.

In October of 1837, just one year after his return to England, he developed the first symptoms of the mysterious illness that was to plague him for almost the rest of his life. The least excitement brought on palpitations of the heart and often stomach pains, nausea, and insomnia. The attacks grew in intensity and frequency, and eventually he became an invalid. His doctors could not understand what was ailing him, nor could they prescribe anything that gave him more than temporary relief. For nearly forty-five years he was not to know one full day of normal living, and his existence became one long struggle with ill-health.

Nothing about his past suggested the possibility of such a crippling disorder. As a boy he had been a sturdy runner, and as a young man he had been a passionate hunter and outdoor man. On the *Beagle* expedition he had gone to some of the roughest and most dangerous places on earth, been one of the hardiest members of the ship's company, and endured extremes of heat, cold, hunger, and thirst. Yet within a few years after his trip around the world this sturdy young man became so sickly that he was forced to give up the active life he loved and retire to the seclusion of his own home.

What was wrong with him? Was it Chagas' disease brought on by his exposure to the bite of the blood-sucking Benchuca bug on one of his Andean expeditions?

The symptoms of Chagas' disease are strikingly similar to those from which Darwin suffered: extreme weariness, intestinal upset, heart spasms, and so on. But there seems, on the other hand, to have been no evidence of the fever and glandular swelling that customarily marks the onset of the illness. Even today, more than one hundred years later, a diagnosis of Chagas' disease can be no more than a shrewd guess that can be neither proved nor disproved.

Sick as Darwin was, he was never so ill that he had to stop work for long periods, and up to his last years he worked harder than many men who enjoy perfectly normal health. In a sense his illness provided the time he needed to do his work. It gave him an excuse to avoid the people he did not want to meet and the social obligations he did not want to keep. In the course of a long lifetime the number of teas, dinners, family gatherings, conferences, club meetings, christenings, births, and funerals he managed to avoid is astounding.

He generally looked well enough, and except when under severe pain was gay and lively. His doctors suspected him of nursing an imaginary illness, and their suspicions caused him even further distress. "Everyone tells me I look quite blooming and most people think I am shamming," he wrote to his friend Joseph Hooker, "but you have never been one of those."

Darwin certainly was not shamming. What, then, was he suffering from?

In the middle of the nineteenth century Darwin and his fellow countrymen lived in a warm, secure world overlooked by God the Father, a personal Being, the Architect of the Universe and the Creator of man, beast, and vegetation. Darwin's revolutionary theory seemed to strike at the heart of this snug view of existence. If the varied species of plants and animals on earth really had evolved on their own, they required no special creator. It was a comfortless, subversive doctrine that appeared to mock at man's fondest hopes and aspirations. Darwin himself said that at the time he formulated the theory he felt as though he were committing a murder.

Yet he was no wild-eyed radical. He was a mild-mannered, modest middle-class young Englishman who only a few years before had been laughed at by the younger officers aboard the *Beagle* for quoting the Bible to defend his position in an argument. The last thing he wanted to do was defy society. Twenty long years were to go by before he reluctantly announced his discovery to the world, and he did so then only because otherwise another man would have taken the credit from him.

Despite his hesitation he did finally reveal his thoughts about evolution to the world, but there must have been other thoughts and feelings buried deep within him that he could never reveal even to himself.

Charles Darwin had been reared by an autocratic father in a home lacking in warmth. He was thrust at an early age into a school that was equally cold and indifferent. There was one way to his father's favor—academic success. And it was precisely in this area that he failed so miserably.

Very early in life he must have developed the feeling that he was unworthy, good—in the damning words he never forgot—only for "shooting, dogs, and rat-catching."

He became shy and retiring, and avoided disagreement and controversy. As he had not dared speak in his father's presence as a small boy, so he feared to assert himself in public in his later years.

Much as he had suffered, he could never bring himself to believe that his father could be anything else than, in his own words, "absolutely right, true and wise." The resentment and anger any child feels at some time or other toward a parent remained bottled up within him. "My father, the kindest man I ever knew," he once wrote, referring to the rat-catching remark, "must have been angry with me when he used these words."

It would not have been easy for any son, let alone one as sensitive and gentle as Charles, to rebel against a father like Robert Darwin. Harsh and domineering as he was, he was also indulgent to a fault with his children. Bitterly disappointed in his elder son Erasmus, he nevertheless supported him in grand style all his life. Though he thoroughly disapproved of the *Beagle* venture, he financed the entire undertaking for

Charles. Then, when Charles married, he settled a fortune on him and bought him a home in the country.

Some students of Darwin think that his illness arose out of an inner conflict between his undoubted and touching reverence for his father and his suppressed hostility toward him. Out of guilt for feelings he could not consciously express grew a severe and lifelong neurotic disability.

If we accept such a diagnosis of neurotic illness, we still have not ruled out the possibility that he also suffered at the same time from an organic ailment, Chagas' disease or some other chronic illness that he may have picked up on his world-wide travels. The patient who was so anxious that the world should not suspect him of pretending may actually have been the victim of a combination of illnesses.

What is so remarkable about Darwin is that, despite all his anxieties and physical discomfort, he was able to accomplish so much in the course of his lifetime. He never succumbed to self-pity or allowed his handicaps to obstruct his work. His weaknesses do not darken but rather illuminate his heroic stature.

In July of 1837 Darwin began to jot down his first thoughts on evolution, and by October of that year he had already developed the symptoms of his illness. "I have not been so well of late with an uncomfortable palpitation of the heart," he wrote to Henslow "and my doctors urge me strongly to knock off all work." Did the dread of his forthcoming battle with authority trigger off the mysterious malady? It may be more than coincidence that his thoughts about evolution and his symptoms should have arisen at the same time.

At the age of twenty-eight, then, we find Charles Darwin settled down in London, a young naturalist who had found his

Charles Darwin about the time of his marriage to Emma Wedgwood. Charles had thought Emma would reject him because he was too plain.

lifework, groping toward the theme that was going to have such an overwhelming effect on the world. The time had come for him to think of marriage. There could be no doubt that he was going to marry a Wedgwood. His father had married a Wedgwood; his sister Caroline had married a Wedgwood. For Charles the only question was: which one?

At the moment there was only one available: Emma, one year older than Charles, tall, slender, brown-haired and gray-eyed, patiently waiting for him at Maer ever since he had stepped off the gangplank at Falmouth Harbor. At twelve she had been nicknamed Miss Slip-Slop; she would be the kind of wife who would never be distressed by his slovenly habits or his crateloads of specimens scattered about the house. She would have no objection at all to a husband who devoted his life to Megatherium, Toxodon, beetles, spiders, barnacles, or seashells.

On a bright Sunday in November, 1838, the London bachelor hesitantly went up to Maer full of tormenting self-doubt because he feared he was too plain-looking. To his surprise, Emma accepted him at once.

They were married in Maer Church on January 29, 1839, and moved to a small house at 12 Upper Gower Street in London with a little garden just "big enough for a mouthful of clean air." Two vanloads of specimens from Charles's *Beagle* days came along with them, with more to follow. With the money Emma brought to the marriage, and the estate of £13,000 that Dr. Darwin generously settled on his son, the young couple was free from all financial worries.

They were hardly inside the door before Emma discovered that she had married a sick man. Undisturbed, she got down at once to taking care of her husband. As someone observed, it turned out to be the case of the perfect nurse marrying the perfect patient. William Erasmus, the first of their ten children, was born at the end of the year and nicknamed Mr. Hoddy-Doddy. "He is so charming," the doting father wrote to a friend, "I defy anyone to say anything in his praise of which we are not fully conscious."

The most affectionate and tender of parents, Darwin could also observe his children with the detachment of the scientist. Of William he wrote: "During the first seven days reflex actions such as sneezing, hiccupping, yawning, stretching, sucking and screaming were well-performed by my infant. On the seventh day I touched the sole of his foot with a bit of paper and he jerked it away at the same time curling his toes."

With a growing family and continued ill-health, London living proved too much for Darwin, and he purchased a house, with funds provided by his father, in the village of Downe in Kent, less than twenty miles to the south of the city. Called Down, the whitewashed brick house stood three stories high, solid and honest. It was about a quarter of a mile from the center of the village, a small community of three little streets converging on a modest flint-rock church.

Though only a short distance from London, the village was quite isolated, for the only means of transportation was by stagecoach and, later, by way of one train a day from Croydon, ten miles off. The surrounding countryside was a patchwork of quiet plowed fields separated by shaws, or straggling strips of woods, with a line of gentle chalk hills to the south. Today there is still no direct public conveyance to the city, and the valley, with its old houses, hedgerows of holly trees, and meadows in which horses graze, holds fast to its rural isolation.

On September 14, 1842, Darwin left London and moved to Downe, where he was to spend the rest of his life, accompanied by his little family, his collection, his assorted ailments, and the idea that was to change the thinking and the attitudes of modern man.*

---

* His home, now a public museum, is open daily except Fridays. The house is furnished very much as Darwin left it. In the pleasant, uncluttered drawing room is the grand piano on which Emma used to play for Charles, and the settee on which he rested. In the Old Studio, where he did most of his work, are his tools and equipment: geological hammer, microscope, drawing board, and even part of his beetle collection. As you stand in the drawing room and look out through the large windows at the flowerbed, the green lawn, and the patch of woods in the distance, you could for a moment believe that Darwin was about to enter and greet you.

To reach Down House from London, take the Green Bus from Victoria Station and then transfer to the Red Bus at Keston Church. Darwin's home is a pleasant ten-minute walk from the center of Downe.

8

I perceived that selection was the keystone of man's success in making useful races of plants and animals.

CHARLES DARWIN

The Keystone

Darwin was a wealthy man who could have lived in retirement, pursuing his hobbies, calling on his neighbors, caring for his ever-growing family, and in general enjoying the leisurely existence of a country gentleman. But the need to demonstrate the truth of evolutionary theory drove him on, forced him, despite his debilitating illness, into regular habits of work, and never permitted him a day of idleness.

He had to find out how evolution worked. What led to changes in species? Why did some groups of animals and plants appear? Why did some disappear? Unless he could find a coherent explanation of how the process operated, he was just a spinner of theories, a player of hunches, a dabbler like his grandfather Erasmus, certainly not a scientist. "From my early youth," he wrote, "I have had the strongest desire to understand or explain what I observed." There must be a hidden meaning, an underlying law that bound together what he had observed on the *Beagle* voyage. He sought it now.

Lamarck had already proposed an explanation for the evolution of the forms of life: need and use. Snails developed tentacles to feel out their surroundings, snakes their long bodies to get through narrow passages. Moles became blind because they did not need the use of their eyes underground. Giraffes acquired their extraordinary necks by browsing on the tallest branches of trees, and shorebirds grew their long legs by wading in water.

"The shorebird," Lamarck wrote, "wishing to act so that it will not fall into the water will develop the habit of extending and lengthening its feet. Hence it will result in generations of birds which continue to live in this manner so that the individuals find themselves raised as if up on stilts on long naked feet."

Lamarck believed in the inheritance of acquired characteristics: that the shorebird, for example, passed on to its offspring the increased leg length it had acquired within its own lifetime. The process was slow and cumulative, each generation contributing a small share to the changes that finally produced a new species. It was as though families of blacksmiths, by practicing their trade over many generations, ultimately developed a mighty-muscled race.

Darwin impatiently pushed Lamarck aside. Though the French zoologist's imagination was bold, his facts were meager. He assumed the truth of his conclusions without undertaking to prove them. What Darwin was after was solid scientific evidence on which to build a theory.

There was plenty of evidence right under his nose. Every day men were breeding new varieties of pigs, sheep, cows, fish, birds, and plants. Hundreds of different kinds of dogs had been bred from ancestors. Horses as different as the ponderous Percheron and the sleek Arabian were derived from an Asiatic pony ancestor. "We may suppose," Darwin wrote, "that men of one district required swifter horses while those of another required stronger horses. The early differences would be very slight but in the course of time . . . would become established into two distinctive breeds."

Breeding began in prehistoric times when men first learned to domesticate wild animals and plants. In primitive regions of the world men were still improving the breeds of animals in much the way their ancestors had done. The Indians on Tierra del Fuego had said to Darwin: "Old woman no use; dog hunt otter." In other words, when times were hard they killed off the old women of the tribe so that there would be enough food for the dogs. When famine struck, and they had to destroy even the dogs, they tried to save the strongest and most intelligent. By continuing this kind of selection over many generations, they ultimately produced an improved variety of hunting dog.

Today the professional breeder creates new varieties by deliberate selection. We glance at a flock of pigeons, and they all look alike to us. The pigeon fancier, however, is sensitive to variations, however slight, whether in shape of head, breadth of shoulders, length of wing, details of tail feathers, or color of eye. He carefully selects for mating only those birds that will breed the quality he is seeking. Domestic varieties of pigeons differing widely in shape, size, structure, and behavior are descended from the wild rock pigeon.

The breeder can create new varieties only because individuals are never exactly alike. We have never found two identical oaks, spiders, blue jays, codfish, cabbages, hogs, tomatoes, or fingerprints. Life has an extraordinary capacity for *variation*. The breeder selects from the variations already available, and accumulates those variations through a number of generations. He emphasizes differences that are already in existence. The cumulative effect of artificial selection eventually yields the Great Dane, the fantail goldfish, the Merino sheep, the Brahman cow, the nectarine, the Shasta daisy, and new breeds of corn.

At this point in his thinking Darwin took one of those remarkable leaps forward that became the hallmark of his genius. If artificial selection could produce new varieties of plants and animals, could there possibly be a natural agency, a kind of natural selection, that brought new species into the world? But having come so far, he could not go on. He could not imagine how selection could possibly apply to nature.

In October, 1838, he happened to pick up a little book, by the political economist Thomas Malthus, called *Essay on the Principle of Population*. He read it, as he said, for amusement, but before he was through he knew he held in his hand the answer he was seeking.*

In his essay Malthus develops an idea he derived from none other than America's Benjamin Franklin, scientist, statesman, diplomat extraordinary, author of *Poor Richard's Almanac,* founder of the first public library, fire department, and post office in the Colonies, and inventor of the Franklin stove, lightning rod, grocer's claw, and bifocal lenses. Franklin not only "drew the lightning from out the skies," but through Malthus contributed an idea important to evolutionary theory.

In the absence of any restriction, plants and animals, Franklin once observed, will keep on increasing in number until they overrun the planet. If no other plant existed than fennel,

---

* The *Essay* is short, sprightly, easy to read, and highly provocative. Before you are through, you may find yourself in fighting disagreement with the author.

fennel would soon overspread the earth. If there were no other people than the English, the English in a few ages would occupy all the habitable regions of the globe. But there are plants other than fennel and men other than the English, and their crowding and interference with one another keep their numbers in check.

Malthus took this homely observation of Franklin much further. He contended that there never could be enough food for all human beings because the production of food can never keep up with the number of people born to consume it. It is a kind of vicious circle from which mankind can never hope to escape. "Population when unchecked," he wrote, "increases at a geometric ratio. Subsistence increases only in an arithmetic ratio." That is, if population increased in a ratio of 1, 2, 4, 8, 16, 32, and so on, the supply of food required to support that population would increase only in ratio of 1, 2, 3, 4, 5, 6, and so on.*

When population goes beyond the means that can support it, men are forced into a savage competition for the bare necessities of life, and the consequence is famine, poverty, disease, and war. "I can see no way out by which man can escape from the weight of this law," concluded Malthus, thereby dooming mankind to hardship and misery forever.

Malthus's dire prophecies did not impress Darwin. What struck him was the picture of a universal struggle for existence among all organisms, not only man, because of limitations on food and space. All life under favoring circumstances tended to increase at an enormous rate. In South America Darwin had seen vast herds of wild horses swarming over the

---

* Here Malthus's logic is shaky. If man can increase in a geometric ratio, there is just as much reason to suppose that plants and animals can also do so.

ampas, all of them descended from a handful of strays that had wandered away from the first Spanish settlements. Were their food supply unlimited and natural enemies absent, these horses would soon overrun the continent.

"Every organic being," Darwin wrote, "increases at so high a rate that if not destroyed the earth would soon be covered by the progeny of a single pair. If a plant produced only two seeds—and no plant is so unproductive—and the seedlings next year produced only two and so on, in twenty years a million plants would be descended from the two original seeds." The elephant is the slowest breeder of all animals, yet if all its children lived, after a period of 750 years there would be nearly 19 million elephants alive descended from just one pair. Man is also a slow breeder. Nevertheless his numbers tend to double every twenty-five years. At such a rate, in less than one thousand years there would "literally not be standing room for his children."

Why, then, has the earth not been overrun by horses, elephants, seeds, or men? Because, said Darwin, their increase is held in check by a struggle for existence.

By the struggle for existence he had far more in mind than the picture of two wolves battling to a bloody death over a scrap of meat. Survival frequently depends on peaceful rather than on aggressive traits, such as the ability to cooperate or to utilize whatever food or water is available. A desert plant, for example, struggles for existence when it competes with its neighbors for its share of water. Fruit trees whose survival depends on the dissemination of seed may be said to struggle with each other "in tempting birds to devour" the fruit and hence spread the seed. The struggle is often keenest between allied species because they are competing for the same food or space. A new species of swallow, when introduced to a territory, often drives off the native bird.

Every time a population expands, the struggle for survival is intensified. Untold millions perish without ever coming to maturity.

But some do survive. What is there about them that they survive while others fall by the wayside?

And it was at this point in his thinking that Darwin took his leave of Malthus and of everyone who had ever thought about evolution. His answer became the foundation of his grand design. Here is how he put it:

"As many more individuals of each species are born than can possibly survive and as consequently there is a frequently recurring struggle for existence, it follows that any being if it vary, however slightly, in any manner profitable to itself . . . will have a better chance of surviving and thus be naturally selected. From the strong principle of inheritance any selected variety will tend to propagate its new and modified form."

Under the highly competitive conditions of nature, then, only the better adapted or favored will grow to adulthood and pass their favorable characteristics on to their offspring. Or stated more precisely: those variations will be preserved that increase the individual's ability to leave fertile offspring. Given a sufficient number of generations, species would change or evolve.*

At last Darwin had his agency—which he called "natural

---

* Darwin stood Malthus on his head. For Malthus the highly competitive conditions of life led, at least for mankind, to increasing misery. For Darwin they led to improvement and progress by way of evolution.

election"—that performed the same function as the breeder.
What man has been able to accomplish in a few thousand
years, Darwin argued, certainly nature should have been able
to bring about in the millions of years life has been on this
earth. In the forthcoming years he was to trace out the many
ramifications of his theory and give it the solid scientific frame-
work from which it has never been shaken.

In 1844, a book called *Vestiges of the Natural History of
Creation* suddenly appeared in which the author boldly cham-
pioned the cause of evolution, although he dared not place his
name on the title page. So well did the journalist Robert
Chambers hide his identity that no one suspected he was the
author until forty years later.

The book aroused a tremendous storm of controversy and
bitter opposition and gave Darwin a taste of what was bound
to occur when he let the world know what he was doing at
Down House.

Yet *Vestiges of the Natural History of Creation* was a very
mild-mannered and essentially pious book in which God the
Almighty did not deign to stoop to separate acts of creation
but permitted higher forms of life to rise out of lower.
Chambers weakened his argument with errors of fact and old
wives' tales about life arising out of nonlife, asserting, for
example, that clover in the absence of seed sprang spontaneously from earth spread with lime.

Mr. Vestiges, as the author was called, was criticized not
only by the orthodox but also by Darwin because he had provided no agency to bring evolution about except a vague im-
pulse toward improvement in nature and the good will of God.

Darwin shrugged off a theory that made a personal deity responsible for the origin of plants and animals. No longer able
to accept an account of creation that was patently contradicted

by the facts of geology, he was gradually abandoning his religious faith. "The Old Testament was no more to be trusted," he declared, "than the sacred books of the Hindoos. . . The fact that many false religions have spread over the earth like wildfire" made him doubt the truth of his own.

In the mid-nineteenth century new discoveries in the natural sciences came thick and fast, and each one of them seemed aimed at the authority of the Bible. Jacques Boucher de Crèvecœur Perthes, the French amateur anthropologist, in 1838, discovered flint axes and arrowheads belonging to people that had lived when animals long extinct had flourished in Europe. The first fossil skull of an extinct type of man was found in 1848 in a quarry on the Rock of Gibraltar and then confirmed eight years later by similar discoveries in the Neanderthal Valley in Germany. It was becoming increasingly difficult to believe that man had come into existence only six thousand years before in the Garden of Eden.

With each discovery people felt that their deepest religious and moral convictions were being undermined. Principles of science that today appear in most secondary-school biology texts were then received with soul-searching anxiety. Darwin was not the only one who felt a deep sense of guilt in abandoning the Biblical account of creation. "If only the geologists would let me alone," wailed the young English writer John Ruskin. "At the end of every verse in the Bible I hear the clink of their hammers."

Yet in time people learned to tolerate the idea of the great age of the earth and even of the antiquity of man. They could not, however, part with the belief that God had personally intervened in the world to establish each species of plant and animal. To deny God's role as the creator of species seemed to deny His very existence.

As far as Darwin was concerned, a man's religion was his own affair, and he tried to keep his loss of faith to himself. He shrank from argument about any topic, let alone religion. But what of Emma? Should he tell his young wife he no longer believed? He consulted his father, and the cunning old man, who had made a lifelong practice of hiding his own agnostic attitude from his family, advised his son to keep his doubts to himself.

But Emma eventually learned the truth, and when she did she was deeply troubled. To the end of their days together she urged on Charles the consolation of religion. Yet she never upbraided him. "Everything that concerns you concerns me," she wrote. "I should be most unhappy if I thought we did not belong to one another."

Never did a man devote himself so completely to one goal. From the time he read Malthus until his death forty-four years later, Darwin centered all his work on natural selection. Despite his invalidism he carried on a tremendous burden of work, maintained a vast correspondence, did countless experiments, and wrote a good many books. Down House became his laboratory and workroom, a one-man scientific institute.

Since Darwin was at home almost all the time, his children came to think of him as a special kind of playmate, who could be called upon at any time to entertain them. At the age of four one of his sons, meeting a little resistance, offered him a penny bribe to drop his work and come outside to play. The child of an aloof and forbidding parent, Darwin must have determined to give to his own children the love and companionship he never had in his own childhood.

He often entertained his children with stories of his youth, and his adventures aboard the *Beagle* became as familiar to them as if they too had shipped out of Plymouth Harbor on the voyage around the world. When his boys took up beetle hunting, he took as much pride in their finds as though he were again building his own collection at Shrewsbury. All of them were amateur natural scientists at one time or another, and insisted upon becoming their father's assistants. They were in and out of his study all day long, looking over his shoulder, poking through his specimens, or picking out for themselves tape, glue, micrometers, or magnifying glasses. As often as they invaded his workroom, he could not bring himself to scold or punish.

Once, coming upon Leonard, the baby of the family at the time, jumping up and down on a brand-new sofa, all the indulgent father could say was, "Oh, Lenny, Lenny, that's against all rules." To which Lenny replied, "Then I think you'd better go out of the room." Lenny was probably echoing the direst threat he had ever heard from his father.

Darwin had a strong sentimental streak in him that persisted throughout his life. When his children grew older and began to address him formally as "Father," he was broken-hearted. Why not "Poppa" just as when they were babies? "Might as well call me *dog*," he vainly protested.

Surprisingly, Darwin sent his boys to "public schools" of the type of Shrewsbury where he had passed so many miserable years of his own childhood. "No one can more truly despise the old stereotyped classical education than I do," he wrote apologetically, "but yet I have not had the courage to break through the trammels." At heart the great rebel remained a conventional middle-class gentleman, anxious to conform to the demands of his society.

Darwin's feeling of tenderness toward his family extended to all living things. No coachman dared drive his team at a fast clip past the door of Down House for fear Darwin would upbraid him for mistreating his horses. He had a fondness even for his plants, on occasion stroking them gently just as though they were household pets. In describing his specimens he sometimes sounded, as his children were quick to point out, as though he were writing advertisements for them. In *The Origin of Species* he cannot restrain his admiration for a barnacle "with six pairs of beautifully constructed natatory legs, a pair of magnificent compound eyes and extremely complex antennae."

The contemporary picture of the research worker in his white-walled immaculate laboratory would never apply to Charles Darwin. Never was there a scientist who performed his labors under more helter-skelter circumstances. The family constantly intruded on him. If a child were ailing, it was not uncommon for him to tuck the boy up on a sofa in his study and take care of him as he worked. His cabinet drawers were all carefully labeled with stickers marked *seeds, pulley wheels, camel hair brushes, screws, cork cutters, matches, razors*, and so on, but when he wanted a specific object he had to go rummaging through all of them because they rarely contained what they were supposed to. He stubbornly held to the belief that once you threw anything away you would want it directly, so that the drawers became filled with odds and ends, most of them quite useless.

At work in his study Darwin customarily used a chair fitted with wheels that had belonged to his father. While seated in the chair he could swing over to a far part of the room and secure a piece of equipment without getting up. His laboratory tools were makeshift: his yardstick was battered and used by everyone in the household; his scale was askew; his two micrometers, as his children discovered to their great glee, gave differing results; jagged pieces of glass were used to cover his specimens. To the end of his life, the great scientist retained the make-do manner of the amateur. He never got over the habits of the small boy in the garden shed at Shrewsbury playing at chemistry with his big brother.

In 1842, Darwin wrote out a thirty-seven page outline of his views on evolution. Two years later came a 230-page expansion of his ideas to which he attached a letter to Emma giving her solemn instructions as to its disposition were he to die. "It is my belief," he prophetically wrote, "that some day this sketch will be a considerable step in science. Were I to die suddenly before completing this work I am assigning four or five hundred pounds for the editing and publishing of it." Then he listed a number of editors who might be responsible for its publication, with the name of Charles Lyell leading all the rest.

In point of fact this 230-page manuscript was not a sketch but a remarkably complete presentation of the arguments and facts in support of evolution and natural selection. According to Sir Julian Huxley, one of the most distinguished biologists in the world today and the grandson of Thomas Huxley, the great champion of Darwin, the publication of the 1844 abstract would have had the same revolutionary effect on the world as *The Origin of Species,* which was not published until fifteen years later.

At this point one would imagine that Darwin would get down to his great task at once. Instead, as though some powerful genie were holding him back, he pushed his "sketch" aside, showing it to no one but his friend Joseph Hooker, and turned to a book called *Geological Observations in South America* and then to a revision of *The Voyage of H.M.S. 'Beagle.'*

When these two books were completed, he discovered he

Joseph Hooker, distinguished naturalist and Darwin's constant good friend. He later became director of the Kew Botanic Gardens in London.

must do a bit of research on the barnacles of Chile, the entire project to take only a few months. But once having taken hold, he could not let go. Continuously plagued by self-doubt he had to run down the most trivial fact; he had to know as much about the subject as any human being could possibly know. He begged and borrowed barnacles from all over the globe, and eventually had over ten thousand at hand. So completely did he immerse himself in his task that his children got the idea that every other father was engaged in the same work, and one of his sons asked a neighbor's boy, "When does your father do his barnacles?"

What began as a casual study of one kind of barnacle blossomed into a full-scale worldwide investigation of almost all the varieties of these little creatures. Even today, more than a century later, Darwin's two volumes are still the standard reference on the subject. Eight long years went by before Darwin was at last satisfied. The project was over, and the specimens that had cluttered the house so long were shipped out. His reward was twofold: the receipt of the medal of the Royal Society, one of the highest honors of British science, and the understanding the study had given him of the overwhelming degree of variation that exists in nature. Even in the same species of these obscure crustaceans he had discovered evidence of considerable variation within many of the species.

Nothing now stood in the way of getting to work on his great book.

9

I never did pick anyone's pocket but . . . I kept on feeling just as if I were stealing from you.

CHARLES DARWIN TO JOSEPH HOOKER

The Origin of Species

Darwin was sometimes so ill that it seemed he could not go on for another day. A thirty-minute conversation with a distant relative was enough to give him a night of pain and sleeplessness. He rarely left the house because social visiting brought on further distress. To conserve his energy he cultivated extremely methodical habits and arranged his daily schedule so that intensive periods for work were relieved by frequent breaks for rest and reading.

Driven not only by suffering but also by fear that others suspected him of shamming, he went from doctor to doctor both for relief and for reassurance that he was really sick. He tried all kinds of treatment, including water therapy and starvation dieting. All worked—as new treatments will—for a time, and then all left him as miserable as before.

A virtual prisoner in his own home, how was Darwin to gather the information he required to establish the validity of his theory of evolution. His experiences on his journey around the world provided a vast storehouse of evidence, but new ques tions arose all the time. To find the answers he enlisted the help of his friends, just as he had called on his classmates to gather beetles for him during his student days at Cambridge. When, in July, 1837, he opened his first notebook on the transmutation or evolution of species, he stood completely alone in the scientific world. Gradually he won over the four outstanding natural scientists of the day: first the vastly talented Joseph Hooker, who was to become director of the Kew Botanic Gardens in London; then the brilliant biologist Thomas Huxley and the American botanist Asa Gray; and finally the great Charles Lyell, whose *Principles of Geology* had started Darwin on the road toward his grand design. *The Origin of Species,* as Darwin's masterwork was eventually called, turned out to be a kind of collaboration, perhaps the first team project in the history of science.

Darwin may have had a reticent manner, but he could be a tyrant in his demands. His letters begging for information ran to thousands of pages. He assigned monumental tasks to his friends: Asa Gray was to report to him on the alpine plants of North America, Hooker on the vegetation of New Zealand, and Huxley on the embryology of fish. Total strangers received requests for specimens such as the "body of a half-breed African cat." Schoolboys were delegated to collect snakes' eggs at the rate of two shillings a dozen.

On the other hand, he probably responded to every appeal he ever received. He would be the delight of any autograph "hound" today. If he failed to answer a letter promptly, his neglect kept him sleepless all night long. Even the foolish young man who wrote to say that he had undertaken to uphold evolution in a debate but had no time or inclination to do any studying and wanted Darwin to supply him with a résumé of his views received a civil response.

It was Darwin's custom to invite his scientist friends to Down House for a day or weekend and then pump them dry. Hooker, honored by an invitation to come for an entire week, quickly discovered that it was not all play: Darwin tackled him every day immediately after breakfast with questions he had already prepared on slips of paper.

Yet his friends never resented his demands. Completely won over by his good nature and modesty, they felt they gained far more from him than they gave. "When he was excited with pleasant talk," Hooker wrote, "his whole manner was wonderfully bright. . . . His laugh was a free and sounding peal like that of a man who gives himself sympathetically and with enjoyment to the person and the thing which has amused him. . . . A more hospitable and attractive house could not be imagined—there were long walks, romps with the children, Darwin's own hearty manner, strolls with him and interviews to discuss any branch of biological and physical knowledge. I always left with the feeling that I had imparted nothing and carried away more than I could stagger under."

By early 1856, more than twenty years after Darwin had first formulated his views about evolution, he still had made no announcement to the world. His friends, led by Lyell, kept urging him to publish, even if it were a "very thin and little volume." In May of that year, egged on by his brother Erasmus, who kept warning him, "You'll find someone will have been before you," Darwin actually sat down to write his masterwork. He titled it *Natural Selection*. No "very thin and little volume," it was to be a monumental book of over 750,000 words that would take many years to complete.

The great plan, however, was never realized, and *Natural Selection* has remained what is probably the greatest "unfinished symphony" in scientific literature. What eventually took its place was the far more modest book the famous *The Origin of Species*.

The first part of *The Origin of Species* was concerned with Darwin's unique contribution to the theory of evolution, the principle of natural selection.

Darwin began with the obvious fact that man has always been capable of altering varieties of plants and animals. He may do so unintentionally, as primitive men do when they

In 1854, at age 45, when this photograph was taken, Darwin was still two years away from actually beginning to write *The Origin of Species*.

save the animals most useful to them and destroy the rest. Or he may do so methodically, as breeders and fanciers do. "There is no reason why the principles that have acted so efficiently under domestication should not have acted under nature." Just as man by breeding will preserve the characteristics he is seeking and thereby produce new varieties, so will nature in the course of the struggle for existence preserve the most favored and create new species.

Among predatory animals, for example, those individuals with the keenest sight, lightest forms, and longest limbs may be the best hunters, and tend to survive during those periods in the year when prey is the most scarce. They will grow to maturity and rear young which may very well inherit the traits that made their parents so successful in the struggle for existence. Each generation will show further and further divergence from the original stock. Eventually, given time and isolation, the descendants may change so much they can no longer breed with the original type. The descendants have evolved into a new species.

But varieties are not species. That man can change varieties, Darwin acknowledged, is not proof that nature can change species. No one has ever witnessed a change of species. Extending over many thousands of years, the process is far too drawn out for man's direct observation. What Darwin did say is that varieties that live apart long enough under different conditions of life may ultimately become different species. The several finch species he found in the Galápagos Archipelago were originally varieties of a single South American ancestor.

If the origin of any species is to be found in the modification of a single ancestral stock, then there is the grand possibility that all species on this earth have had their origin in one common ancestor that came into being when this planet was very young. Evolution becomes a universal phenomenon starting with the simplest forms of life and developing into the most complex. "Whilst this planet has gone on cycling according to the fixed law of gravity from so simple a beginning, endless forms most beautiful and most wonderful have been and are being evolved."

At this point we might consider the difference between *evolution* and *natural selection*. Whereas evolution is the *process* of biological change by which the various species have risen one from another, natural selection is the *mechanism* or chief means by which these changes have been brought about.

In the latter part of *The Origin of Species* Darwin marshaled the evidence for evolution as a *fact* of nature.

One demonstration of the truth of evolution is so obvious that we tend to pay no attention to it: plants and animals are not arranged in haphazard fashion like pebbles tossed up on a beach but in a meaningful design as though they were related to one another. They fall into groups which in turn fall into still larger groups. Monkeys and apes, for example, belong to the order of primates. The primates are contained within the larger class of mammals which include, among others, the rodents, the carnivores, and the hoofed animals. In their turn the mammals form a subdivision of a still larger group, the vertebrates, all of whom share the same general body plan including a spinal column and a central nervous system, although they may be as diverse as lizards, tortoises, finches, Falkland foxes, whales, and capybaras.

The similarities that tie all backboned animals together cannot be accidental. All must have evolved from a common ancestor. Their resemblance is due to their kinship. Their differences are due to their descent—with divergence and modification—from some ancient parentage. To classify animals and plants is to acknowledge a relationship. Or, as Darwin said, "The bind between two or more species . . . has been inherited from a common parent, all true classification being genealogical."

We are struck by another kind of similarity when we compare corresponding organs, the limbs of different mammals, for example. Examined closely, the forelimb of the mole, the foot of the horse, the wing of the bat, and the fin of the porpoise turn out, structurally, to be the *same* organ. We can explain the likeness only by assuming that these diverse animals have all evolved from an early ancestor that possessed the basic limb from which all the rest are derived.

Many creatures possess not only body parts that play a vital part in keeping them alive but also rudimentary organs that may once have been useful but now have no use at all or have become modified to take on new functions. The teeth of whales, the eyes of some animals inhabiting dark caves, the limbs of snakes, and the wings of penguins and ostriches are all rudimentary. One of the most striking examples of such organs discovered since Darwin's time is the vestigial egg tooth of marsupials, pouched animals such as the kangaroo, although seventy-five million years have gone by since it was necessary for marsupials to crack the shell in order to hatch out of the egg in which they were born.

"Rudimentary organs," Darwin suggested, "may be compared with the letters of a word, still retained in the spelling but no longer pronounced, which may serve as a clue to its derivation." The traces of limb bones found in snakes are reminders that snakes are descended from crawling, lizard-like reptiles, records of a former state of things.

Comparison of the unborn young of different animals offers further confirmation of common descent. In their early stages embryos of quite different animals look so startlingly alike that it is often difficult to tell them apart. "In my possession," wrote Darwin, "are two little embryos preserved in spirits whose names I omitted to attach. They may be lizards or small birds or very young mammals so complete is the similarity." The striking resemblance among the embryos of different animals could be explained only on the basis of common ancestry. Like the study of classification and rudimentary organs, embryology abounds in evidence of the evolutionary design of life.

In the course of his argument Darwin often had to confess there was much he did not know; yet with his usual candor he refused to sidestep any challenge. *Variation* was basic to the principle of natural selection. Nevertheless, he had to admit he did not know how variations had come about.*

He quickly acknowledged that one of the most damaging objections to the theory of evolution was the absence of substantial fossil evidence in the rocks. If species had really diverged from one another in the distant past, where were the intermediate forms that had once linked them together?

It was—and to some extent still is—a valid question. Since man himself cannot generally bear direct witness to evolutionary change, he must rely in good part on the fossil record. The record of the rocks was, unfortunately, skimpy. During his exploration of the pampas Darwin himself had helped to

---

* The genetic origin of variation was not established until years after his death. See page 163.

fill in a few of the gaps. But he was the first to admit that the geological record was full of silences. "The crust of the earth," he wrote, "must not be looked at as a well-filled museum but as a poor collection made at hazard and at rare intervals." And then he hastened to add, "The number of specimens is absolutely as nothing compared with the species which have certainly existed in the past."

We know today that Darwin was right. It was the record that was at fault, not the theory. Research since his time has amply documented his argument. We now have an almost complete fossil series of the evolution of the horse, the camel, the elephant, the sea urchin, and a chambered shellfish called the ammonite. We have identified many of the ancient animals that link amphibians, reptiles, and mammals in a line of common descent. The recent sensational discovery of the australopithecines, a very large group of extinct men and near men in Africa that lived from one to two million years ago, has helped to fill in the evolutionary gap between man and his fossil ape ancestors.

"It is amazing," Sir Gavin de Beer, former director of Natural History at the British Museum has said, "that with the meager materials at his disposal Darwin was able to steer a clear course across a largely uncharted sea of ignorance."

Darwin's plan, then, as set forth in *The Origin of Species,* was simple: He assembled a vast body of evidence to prove that animals and plants could not have been separately created but must have evolved from earlier forms by slow change. And along with this evidence he provided a mechanism by means of which these changes could have been brought about: the principle of natural selection.

In the public mind *evolution* is forever linked with Darwin's name. Yet it is the concept of *natural selection* that is his unique contribution and that he himself placed at the very heart of his doctrine. It is natural selection that makes evolution scientifically intelligible by demonstrating that it behaves according to fixed natural laws:

NATURAL SELECTION AND THE ORIGIN OF SPECIES

1. Organisms tend to increase at a higher rate than their food supply. More young are produced than ever reach adulthood.

2. Because the resources of nature are limited, all life must engage in a struggle for existence in which only the most favored will survive.

3. No two individuals are identical. All show variations, however slight, from one another.

4. Some individuals possess variations that are helpful in the competition for survival. These will produce the most offspring.

5. Such offspring tend to inherit some of their parents' traits and pass them on to their children. Each generation will maintain and improve these characteristics, and so diverge further from the original type. Ultimately the new forms are so different in structure and habit from the original, they can no longer breed with them. They may, therefore, be considered a new species.

10

I see no good reason why the views given in this volume should shock the religious feelings of anyone. . . . The greatest discovery ever made (Newton's law of universal gravitation) was also attacked as subversive of religion.

CHARLES DARWIN

"The Most Dangerous Man in England"

For two years Darwin worked at setting his grand design down on paper, and by June 18, 1858, he had completed approximately ten chapters, with years of labor still ahead of him. On that day he received a letter from the East Indies that threatened to destroy the hopes and aspirations of a quarter of a century of thought and effort. His brother's warning had come true: "You will find that someone will have been before you!"

For a number of years Darwin had been exchanging correspondence with a young British naturalist living in Malaysia named Alfred Russel Wallace. There was nothing in Wallace's letters to arouse Darwin's apprehensions. Wallace told about his eight years of travel in the Far East and of an earlier expedition to the Amazon. In one of his replies Darwin had written with his usual generosity toward younger scientists, "I infinitely admire and honor your zeal and courage in the course of cause of natural science and you have my sincere and cordial good wishes for success of all kinds."

119

Alfred Russel Wallace, co-discoverer of the principle of natural selection. Wrote Darwin, "If Wallace had my manuscript sketch written out in 1842, he could not have made a better short abstract. I never saw a more striking coincidence."

Even when Wallace wrote to say that he had become interested in the problem of evolution, Darwin was not alarmed. A good many people by this time were interested—in a general sort of way. Darwin replied that the problem had held his attention for twenty years and that as a matter of fact he was just then engaged in writing a book on it: "It is really impossible to explain my views in a letter, but I have slowly adapted a distinct and tangible idea—whether true or false others must judge." He seemed to suggest that if Wallace had any notion of getting more deeply involved, he was just wasting his time.

Nevertheless, despite Darwin's implied rebuff, Wallace could not help becoming more and more involved in the subject. Forced to stay in bed one day because of a tropical fever, he recalled a book he had read many years earlier. In it the author claimed that the supply of food available in the world could never keep pace with the increase of population, and therefore a fierce struggle for survival must take place. The book was none other than Malthus's *Essay on the Principle of Population,* which had once so profoundly affected Darwin's thinking.

As Wallace tossed about in his fever, he was seized with a sudden conviction: in a struggle for survival "the inferior would be killed off and the superior remain; that is, the fittest would survive. When changes of land or sea or of climate or of food supply or of enemies occurred, it followed that all the changes necessary for the adaptation of the species to the changing conditions would be brought about, and as great changes in the environment are always slow, there would be ample time for the change to be effected by the survival of the best fitted in every generation. . . . The more I thought this over, the more I became convinced that I had at length found the long sought law of nature that solved the problem of the origin of species."

That evening, the moment his fever went down, Wallace began writing out *his* "distinct and tangible idea" and sent it off to Darwin by the first outgoing mail. In an accompanying letter he asked help in getting it published, and said that he hoped that his conclusions would be as new to Darwin as they were to him.

When Darwin received the fateful letter and manuscript at Down, he was stunned. The idea Wallace hoped would be as new to Darwin as it was to him was none other than the principle of natural selection over which he had labored so long. Wallace could not have made a better outline of the theme of the book on which Darwin was now working than if he had been looking over his shoulder. Yet the two men had never met, and Wallace was ten thousand miles away on the other side of the world. For centuries men had observed the same facts of nature and never penetrated the secret of the evolutionary process. Now, in this fateful year of 1858, not one but two investigators, each working by himself, had discovered the solution.

What was Darwin to do? Disregard Wallace's communication and rush into publication himself? Why not? Why should this young interloper without a tenth of his training, dedication, and labor assume the crown for which he had worked so long? He could have swept into print long ago had he been less conscientious and painstaking. Was he now to be robbed of his fame by this bold stranger who called himself "a young man in a hurry"?

Darwin quickly put such thoughts by. Conscience, severe and demanding, took over. Above all, Wallace must never even imagine he had taken anything from him. He'd rather have all his work go up in flames before any man thought he had behaved in a paltry spirit. Far better to renounce all claims to his discovery and begin all over again!

Wallace's communication could not have come at a worse time. June, 1858, was a disastrous month for Darwin. Both his daughter Henrietta and his infant son Charles were seriously ill. In his distress Darwin turned for advice to his two good friends Lyell and Hooker. Without hesitation they said, "Prepare a short sketch of your book for immediate publication."

Darwin absolutely refused. "Is it honorable for me to do so just because I know that another man has discovered the same identical principle? Wallace might very well claim I published only because I wanted to keep the honor all to myself. I always thought I might be forestalled but I fancied I had a grand enough soul not to care but I find myself mistaken and punished."

Lyell and Hooker kept on insisting, and stubbornly Darwin kept on refusing. Finally, however, they came up with a solution that was able to satisfy even Darwin's scruples: Wallace's paper and an outline of Darwin's 1842 paper were to be published together and read before the Linnean Society. (Named after the Swedish botanist Carolus Linnaeus, the Linnean Society was a notable association of British natural scientists.) In this manner both men would receive joint credit for the discovery.

Never in the history of science did co-discoverers act toward each other with greater understanding and generosity. The two might have become bitter rivals squabbling for priority and honors. Instead, each in his own way sought to yield place to the other.

"I shall always maintain," Wallace later wrote to Darwin, "natural selection to be yours and yours alone. You had worked it out in details I had never thought of years before I had a ray of light on the subject, and my paper would never have convinced anybody, whereas your book [*The Origin of Species*] has carried away captive the best men of the age." Darwin simply replied, "Natural selection is as much yours as it is mine."

With the publication of the two papers in 1858, Darwin sat back to await the consequences. After all the years of hesitation and indecision, the world was at last to learn his secret.

Yet nothing happened. The announcement of the discovery created no stir at all. There was no surprise expressed, no shock. When the papers were read before the Linnean Society on July 1st, neither Wallace nor Darwin was present. Wallace was still abroad, and Darwin was at home mourning the death of young Charles. The thirty members present did not seem at all disturbed that they were hearing a statement that completely struck down some of their most cherished beliefs. It was one of the towering moments in the development of man's ideas, and they did not even rise to discuss the occasion. A revolution was taking place under their noses, and they kept on sleeping.

Joseph Hooker, who was at the meeting, supposed that the Old Guard was overwhelmed by the novelty of the idea, and cautiously refrained from fighting back until they could arm themselves with suitable counterarguments. It is more likely that those who were present at the meeting failed to comprehend the significance of what they were hearing.

As the president of the Society, Thomas Bell, wrote in his annual report a few months later: "The year that has passed has not been marked by any of those striking discoveries which at once revolutionize so to speak the department of science on which they bear or which produce a marked impress on the character of any branch of knowledge."

Poor Thomas Bell! Few judgments have ever proved so outrageously wrong.

The Wallace affair finally stung Darwin into further action. The great work that was to have run over 2,500 pages and taken many years to complete was pushed aside, and instead he concentrated on a moderate-sized volume, taking much of the material from what he had already written.

Why had he resisted publication these many years? Fear of offending the religious feelings of others, boyhood memories of his father's disapproval of whatever he attempted, and a strong aversion to public controversy all probably contributed to his reluctance to expose his great theme to the world. At any event, the sluice gates were now wide open. In just a little over thirteen months, scribbling every day in a vile hand as fast as he could, he completed the book that became *The Origin of Species,* probably the most influential work of modern times.

The Origin of Species appeared on November 24, 1859. Prior to publication Darwin, with characteristic modesty, had said to his publisher John Murray, "I feel bound to say in the clearest terms that . . . if you do not think it likely to have a remunerative sale I completely and explicitly free you from your offer."

But he need not have been concerned about Murray. The first edition was sold out on the day of publication. Less than two months later a second edition appeared, and by January of 1860 over 5,000 copies had been sold. Quickly England became aware that a great conflict was in the making.

To a world convinced that the creatures of this planet were the direct descendants of the animals that emerged two by two out of Noah's ark after their miraculous rescue from the Flood, the book came as a tremendous shock. We who have had over a century to absorb the blow are hard pressed to understand the revulsion, disgust, and fear it aroused.

The Origin of Species is a mild, cautious text in natural history, stocked with a massive array of facts and illustrations that demonstrate the descent of species. The tone is that of a Victorian gentleman who is trying to avoid hurting the sensibilities of his readers. Though convinced of the rightness of his views, he is not too sure he is going to persuade others. He candidly admits the existence of logical arguments against his position, and confesses there is much he can still learn.

Yet the world reacted as though the book were a revolutionary call to overthrow all existing governments and institutions. Its author was attacked as blasphemous, immoral, subversive, radical. Battle lines were quickly drawn up, with the vast majority of men, including most of the scientists of the day, in passionate and determined opposition to Darwin. Within the quiet confines of the Linnean Society the members at last woke from their long sleep, and several resigned because Darwin was not expelled forthwith.

The professional attack on Darwin was led by none other than the old geology teacher at Cambridge who had once predicted great fame for his pupil, Professor Adam Sedgwick. Striding at the head of the clerical brigade was Dr. Samuel Wilberforce, the Bishop of Oxford, a powerful molder of public opinion, and the most persuasive orator in Britain. Wilberforce, sometimes known as "Soapy Sam," set out "to smash Darwin" with ridicule. "Darwin claims we are cousins to the vegetable," he wrote. "Shall we insist that turnips are evolving toward man? Yet the closest microscopic examination fails to detect such a tendency."

To Wilberforce and his followers *The Origin of Species* was a horrible abomination that mocked the revealed word of God and the doctrine of man's fall and redemption. God alone was the creator of animals and plants. If life was the product of a blind fumbling force the Darwinians called natural selection, where then was God's place? Did the Almighty become unnecessary? Little wonder that Darwin was denounced as "the most dangerous man in England!" *

Some people found the topic so abhorrent that they tried to push it under the rug. "Let us hope it is not true," said one gentle lady, "but if it is true let us hope it will never be generally known." Or, in the words of Thomas Carlyle, who never hesitated to shout about what he believed in, "A humiliat-

---

* "Considering how fiercely I have been attacked by the orthodox," Darwin once wryly remarked, "it is ludicrous that I once intended to be a clergyman."

ing discovery and the less said about it the better." Thanks, however, to the Darwinians and anti-Darwinians alike, more was said about it than less, and it became one of the principal subjects of discussion and debate in England, America, and on the European continent.

The Church was not entirely united in its opposition to Darwin. A few liberal ministers led by Charles Kingsley, the author of *Westward Ho!* saw no necessary conflict between Darwinism and religion. God did not have to engage in special acts of creation to maintain His place as Supreme Being. "It is just as noble," Kingsley said, "to believe He created forms capable of self-development as to believe He required fresh acts of intervention to fill the gaps He Himself had made." The very fact of evolution, far from denying God's existence, Kingsley maintained, revealed Him grander and more majestic than His worshipers had ever suspected. The miracles in the Bible were child's play compared to the marvelous complexity and interrelationships of nature recorded in *The Origin of Species*. Overawed by the immense range and magnificence of the evolution of life, men might well raise their voices in prayerful thanksgiving, and cry anew: "Oh, Lord, how manifold are Thy works."

In addition to a few daring churchmen like Kingsley, a number of distinguished writers rallied to Darwin's cause. They included the historian Henry Buckle, the novelists George Eliot and Thomas Hardy, and the consistent supporter of liberty in Britain, the political economist John Stuart Mill. But by far the most outstanding champion of Darwin in the months and years of struggle that lay ahead was Thomas Huxley.

The early careers of both men were startlingly similar. Like Darwin, Huxley had studied medicine and gone off on a five-

Thomas Henry Huxley: Darwin's "bulldog." "Every great truth had begun as a heresy."

year cruise on a Royal Navy ship, H.M.S. *Rattlesnake*, commissioned to chart the waters about Australia. His experiences on the voyage, again like Darwin, led him to a lifelong devotion to the biological sciences. On his return to England he gave up medicine and became a professor of natural science at the Government School of Mines in London. A brilliant scholar, he was elected to the Royal Society when he was only twenty-six.

Unlike Darwin, however, Huxley was no shy, retiring hermit but a pugnacious, scrappy public speaker. He called himself "Darwin's bulldog," and the description was fitting. He was quick to pick up a challenge, and tenacious in maintaining an argument. If any man in England was capable of taking on Wilberforce, it was Huxley.

While Darwin remained quietly in the rural solitude of Downe, nursing his ills and pursuing his researches in garden and hothouse, Huxley traveled everywhere, lecturing, debating, and writing. Eventually, almost by himself, he turned the tide of opinion in favor of his master. The most gifted of all popularizers of science, he was able to portray the ideas of Darwin so vividly that even the man in the street easily comprehended them. When he lectured in the United States, he used the geology of the American continent to illuminate the long history of the formation of the earth. Niagara Falls, he asserted, was a great clock measuring out the countless centuries it had taken the water to cut through the rock. The age-old sandstone of Connecticut put to shame the puny 6,000-year calendar of Bishop Ussher. The theory of evolution was vindicated by the discovery of the fossils of ancient horses on the western plains.

All life, Huxley said, from amoeba to man, was composed of the same identical protoplasm. Between the plant and animal kingdoms there was no sharp distinction, one having risen from the other. Even between the living and the nonliving world, the organic and the inorganic, no fundamental difference existed except in the arrangement of molecules.

He did not fear discussing the touchiest subject of all, the origin of man. There was nothing unique about man's beginnings. Man was part and parcel of this world, descended like all the other animals from the simplest forms of life, which in turn were composed of the common materials of the earth.

Huxley never hesitated to spell out his exact position. Every great truth had begun as a heresy. Between Darwin's scientific view of life and the orthodox view there could be no possible reconciliation. If one was true, then the other had to be false. Either species had been specially created or they had risen out of preexisting forms by the operation of natural causes. Throwing down his gauntlet, Huxley cried: "Choose your hypothesis; I have chosen mine!"

Month by month after the publication of *The Origin of Species* the battle grew fiercer. Men quarreled and wrote angry letters to the papers. Denunciatory reviews filled the press. But the winter of 1859–1860 went by, and the principal antagonists had not yet engaged in formal debate. Finally, on April 30, 1860, at a meeting at Oxford University of the British Association for the Advancement of Science, they met face to face.

When word spread that both Wilberforce and Huxley were going to speak, the crowd grew so vast that the meeting had to be rescheduled for the great library, which was soon crammed with almost a thousand spectators. At the appearance of each of the preliminary speakers the undergraduate students booed and yelled, while the remainder of the audience, catching the carnival spirit of the occasion, proceeded to cheer and applaud. The chairman of the meeting, John Henslow, Darwin's old professor at Cambridge and the man who had launched him on his journey round the world, had a hard time keeping order.

The first speakers having been disposed of, the audience sat back to enjoy the fireworks. But the main event almost failed to come off. In disgust Huxley had left the meeting. He had decided that the atmosphere was hardly suitable to a sober scientific presentation of the issues.

As Huxley walked down the street he met Robert Chambers, the author of *Vestiges of the Natural History of Creation*. In the years since the publication of his book, Chambers had become a firm follower of Darwin. He indignantly demanded that Huxley return to the meeting and face Wilberforce.

"I don't see the good of giving up my peace and quiet in order to be pounded by a bishop," said Huxley.

"You are deserting our side," retorted Chambers.

It was all the encouragement Huxley needed. "Oh, well, if you feel that way," he said, "I'll come and take my share of what is going on."

With Huxley and Wilberforce ready to have a go at it, Henslow presiding, Joseph Hooker scheduled to make the concluding remarks, and none other than Darwin's old commander on the *Beagle,* Robert Fitzroy, now Admiral Fitzroy, in the audience, the stage was set for the great debate of the century.

The only member of the cast who was absent was the hero of the drama himself. Darwin was at home, ailing and concerned about two of his children who were seriously ill. And had he and his family all been in blooming health he probably would not have appeared, so distasteful to him was public squabbling and conflict. "I would as soon have died as tried to answer the Bishop in such an assembly," he said later.

Henslow first called on Wilberforce, who whetted his audience's appetite by claiming that surely there must be others better qualified than he to present the side of truth and religion. Pretending to be reassured by shouts of encouragement from the crowd, he proceeded with his customary wit and brilliance, at first playfully and then in grim earnest, to launch into an all-out assault on Darwin. The audience, completely won over, greeted each savage sally with shouts and applause. But as Wilberforce galloped on, Huxley, who had always stood a little in awe of him, realized that the bishop did not know what he was talking about. It was obvious that he had been primed for the meeting and that he had not learned his lesson well.

Finally Wilberforce, overcome by his own eloquence and the heady approval of the crowd, let himself go altogether. Turning about to face Huxley, he inquired with mock courtesy, "I should like to ask the distinguished Professor Huxley a simple question: is it through your grandfather or your grandmother that you claim descent from a monkey?" Whereupon, to a roar of tumultuous laughter and a sea of waving handkerchiefs, he primly took his seat.

Once he was able to quiet the audience, Henslow called upon Huxley to reply.

As Huxley later told the story: "When Wilberforce turned to me with his insolent question I made up my mind to let him have it. I said in an undertone to Sir Benjamin Brodie, who sat next to me, 'The Lord hath delivered him into my hands.' The old gentleman stared at me as though I had taken leave of my senses."

Huxley then turned to the audience. Quietly and gravely, as though he had not heard Wilberforce's offensive remark, he launched into a brief summary of Darwin's ideas, saying that they represented the best explanation science had found for the origin of species up to the present time. Patiently and dispassionately he took up the bishop's arguments, carefully analyzing each one and directing attention to its flaws. He might have been lecturing to one of his own classes at the School of Mines, so objective was his manner. As to man's relation to the animals, he went on, it was not Darwin's intention to establish a direct link between man and the ape. Rather it seemed that both were descended from a common ancestor that had lived in the far past.

It looked as though Huxley were going to let Wilberforce off scot free, but his dander was up, and he ended with words similar to these (exactly what he said was lost in the tumult that rose in a crescendo as he went on):

"I would have no shame in having an ape for a relative, but I would be ashamed to be associated with a man who uses his great gifts to obscure the truth, who deals with scientific questions about which he knows nothing and who distracts his audience by skilled appeals to religious prejudice. If the question were put to me, would I rather have had a miserable ape for my grandfather or such a man, I should settle for the ape."

Whereupon a great uproar arose, bitter arguments broke out all over the hall, men jumped to their feet shaking their fists at each other, and a lady fainted and had to be carried out. Above the pandemonium could be heard the stern voice of Admiral Fitzroy. Holding an enormous Bible high above his head, he expressed his bitter disappointment in his old shipmate and then appealed to everyone present to reject human institutions for the Word of God as revealed in the Good Book.

Somehow or other order was eventually reestablished, and Henslow called on Hooker for the concluding remarks. Furious at the unfair attack on both Darwin and Huxley, Hooker condemned Wilberforce for not knowing what he was talking about, and accused him of never having read the book he so freely criticized. So ended the historic meeting of April 30, 1860.

Despite Huxley's brilliant presentation and Hooker's "assist," the meeting marked no triumph for Darwin. That the orthodox should remain unconvinced was to be expected, but it was surprising that the scientific community, outside Darwin's immediate supporters, continued to maintain its hostility. Opposition ranged all the way from those who insisted that Darwin had added nothing to what Lamarck had already pointed out to the naturalist who said to Darwin, "Ay, sir, if ye had only stopped with the *Voyage of the 'Beagle.'* " One zoologist told Darwin that though he might read the *Origin*, he would never believe it. Professor Adam Sedgwick, whom Darwin had once accompanied on a geological tour of Wales, wrote: "I have read your book with more pain than pleasure. Parts I admired; other parts I read with absolute sorrow because I think them utterly false and grievously mischievous. . . . There is a moral part of nature as well as a physical. A man who denies this is deep in the mire of folly. . . . I humbly accept God's revelation of Himself and do my best to act in conformity of that knowledge which He alone can give me. If you and I do this we shall meet in Heaven."

Apparently Sedgwick did not anticipate an encounter in heaven with his old hiking partner but had quite another destination in mind for him, for he followed this letter some months later with a rabid attack on the *Origin* in the *Spectator,* one of England's most influential magazines.

Even within the Darwin camp there were occasional wavering and backsliding. Charles Lyell, Darwin's good friend and teacher, hesitated from time to time in his acceptance of the evolution of species. Though there were short spells when Darwin himself lost heart, the sick man of Down, despite the hostility of old friends, the uncertainty of followers, and the constant attacks in the press, continued on his way undeterred.

"I fully believe," he wrote to Hooker, "that our cause will prevail."

Part III

Homecoming

The years from 1860 to 1871 were crucial for Darwin. While his champions fought valiantly, his enemies struck back in every arena of public life. "What an accursed evil," Darwin wrote, "all this quarreling within what ought to be the peaceful realm of science."

There was too much at stake for Darwin to stand aside. From Down House went out a constant series of letters cheering on his followers, replying to hostile reviews, and enlisting and encouraging new allies. Gradually the scales tipped in his favor. In the face of bitter opposition Darwin in 1864 received the Copley Medal of the Royal Society, Britain's highest honor in the field of science. What pleased him more than the acknowledgment was that Charles Lyell took the occasion to announce his conversion to the truth of evolution. Master and pupil had changed places.

Before Darwin could triumph, however, he had to convince his fellowmen that they too were part of the grand design he had outlined in *The Origin of Species*. Man must yield his fabled abode in heaven and find his home here on earth, brother to all living things.

11

Man with all his noble qualities—with sympathy which feels for the most debased, with benevolence which extends not only to other men but also to the humblest living creatures, with his godlike intellect which has penetrated into the movements and constitution of the solar system— with all these exalted powers man still bears in his bodily form the indelible stamp of his lowly origin.

CHARLES DARWIN

The Evolution of Man

One hundred years ago most men and women living in the Western World believed that they were the children of Adam and Eve, the divine couple created by God. In the decade following the publication of *The Origin of Species,* people grew to accept the doctrine of evolution as far as plants and animals were concerned, but they could not go all the way and give up the notion of man's special creation.

The question Wilberforce flung at Huxley was stupid and arrogant, but he had put his finger on a problem that disturbed all sensitive men: are we really part of the animal world, kin to the swimming, crawling, flying, tree-swinging creatures of this planet? Darwin fully appreciated the resistance to the idea of man's evolution. In the *Origin* he had discreetly said nothing about it except to predict that someday "light will be thrown on the origin of man and his history."

Someday? When would that day come, and who would throw the light? Darwin? He would have liked to avoid the

137

whole topic. To publish a book on man while the public was still struggling with the *Origin* would create so much additional ill-feeling that natural selection could never get a fair hearing. With victory within his grasp, why stir up new antagonisms? The very thought probably made him more ill. Had he not done his duty to science? Let younger and stronger men now take up the burden.

In his dilemma Darwin appealed to Wallace, pressing his notes and references on him. Would Wallace write such a book? "I have been so steadily going downhill, I cannot help doubting whether I can ever crawl uphill again." But Wallace, busy at the time with a book about his travels in the East Indies, was unmoved.

Darwin put *man's descent* aside as he had once pushed the *origin of species* aside. He would investigate a field that was free of denunciation and controversy, something innocent and safe, orchids, for example.

Orchids were plentiful in the countryside about Downe. They fascinated Darwin because of the unusual adaptations they showed. An adaptation is a body structure or manner of behaving that ensures that an organism will thrive in its particular environment. The woodpecker's stiff prop-like tail, which keeps it from falling from its perch on the side of a tree, its long stout beak for chiseling holes into bark, and its long tongue for scooping out grubs are all adaptations.

Darwin discovered that some orchids possess the most amazing adaptations to secure cross-fertilization, the transmission of pollen from one plant to another. The Coryanthes orchid has a lower lip hollowed out into a bucket which is half-filled with fluid. Bumblebees frequently push each other into the bucket. As a bee crawls out along a narrow spout it becomes covered with a sticky mass of pollen. Flying to another flower, it tumbles into the bucket, crawls out along the narrow passage, and rubs up against the stigma, the part of the female organ of a plant that receives the pollen. "We see," said Darwin, "the full use of every part of the flower, the bucket half-full of water that prevents the bees from flying away and forces them to crawl along the spout and rub against the pollen masses and then fertilize the next flower with which they come into contact."

The orchid with the most improbable contrivance of all is the Catasetum. When a bee visits this flower, it disturbs a long tapering projection, or antenna. A vibration is transmitted to a membrane that ruptures and sets free a "spring" that at once shoots a mass of pollen into the air. The pollen lands on the back of the insect, which then flies off and fertilizes the next flower it visits. The "spring" is powerful enough to catapult a mass of pollen several yards.*

Darwin once received an orchid from Madagascar with a nectar tube over eleven inches long. A nectar tube holds the sweet fluid that attracts insects to a flower, and therefore ensures their coming into contact with the pollen. But what insect had a proboscis long enough to get to the bottom of this extraordinary tube? And if no such insect existed, what was the function of such an amazing adaptation? Darwin reasoned that the orchid could never have evolved into its present form unless there was an insect that could get at its nectar. He was right. A moth was subsequently discovered with a coiled proboscis that was able to unroll to just the required length. The coordination between a flower and the insect that

---

* To Hooker, who had been supplying the specimens for his experiments, Darwin wrote: "If you can spare another Catasetum I should be most grateful. . . . A cursed insect or something let my last flower off last night."

helps to fertilize it is as delicate as that between a lock and key.

Color is another type of adaptation that attracts insects to plants. Darwin shrewdly noted that the seeds of plants that are not gaily colored, grasses for example, are not carried by insects but by the wind. The lovely appearance of a plant is as much a device for attracting insects as its nectar. What we human beings think of as beauty in a flower is actually an adaptation for securing cross-fertilization.

Why does nature, so to speak, go to such lengths to achieve cross-fertilization? The result of fertilization is the production of seed, and seed can also be produced by self-fertilization, that is, by the passage of pollen from the male to the female organ of the *same* plant. The vital discovery Darwin made was that the offspring of cross-fertilization are stronger, larger, and more fertile than those of self-fertilization. Adaptations that assure cross-unions confer a tremendous advantage on plants.

Adaptation was a sensitive subject in the middle of the nineteenth century, with important religious overtones. The color and scent of flowers, the long tongue of the woodpecker, the webbed feet of wading birds, or the pouch of kangaroos were regarded, not as chance products of nature, but as inventions of God, testifying to His existence and wisdom.

Anyone who examined the amazingly intricate contrivances by which plants were fertilized might well conclude that someone had carefully planned and designed them. As William Paley, the early nineteenth-century English theologian, urged: as a watch is unthinkable without a watchmaker, so an adaptation must testify to the existence of Him who created it. "Design must have a designer; that designer must be God."

Darwin, however, viewed adaptations through another winlow. These inventions did not indicate that plan or design operated in the world but merely demonstrated that some variations had survival value. Plants and animals that failed to evolve suitable responses to the struggle for existence simply did not live and produce offspring. Under the direction and pressure of natural selection, only those that adapted to their environment survived.

The universe as Darwin saw it gave no evidence of either kindness or design. "There is too much misery in the world," he wrote. "I am inclined to look at everything as resulting from laws with the details whether good or bad left to the working out of what we may all call chance. . . . The lightning kills a man whether a good or a bad one owing to the complex action of natural law."

Darwin's orchid book, *On the Various Contrivances by which British and Foreign Orchids Are Fertilized by Insects,* was published in 1862 and was favorably received by a public unaware that the book provided further evidence of the power and scope of natural selection. "No one has perceived," Darwin gleefully wrote to Asa Gray in America, "that my chief interest in my orchid book has been that it was a flank attack on the enemy."

The orchid book out of the way, Darwin now turned to another "safe" volume, *The Variation of Animals and Plants Under Domestication,* which he completed at the beginning of 1867. Now at last he was ready to take up *his* task, the origin of man. It was a topic that had held his mind from the first day he had thought about evolution.

Thirty years earlier he had written in his notebook: "Man in his arrogance thinks himself a great work worthy of the interposition of the deity. More humble I believe and truer to consider him created from animals." His new book, *The*

Descent of Man, was to present this daring and sacrilegious view of the world. His hesitation was prompted by more than his customary aversion to public controversy. He had learned to live with the hostility of the outside world, but there was also opposition closer at hand. His own dear wife was very pious, and submitted to the many sorrows that befell her because she knew that suffering was meant to help her look forward to a future life in heaven. She attended church regularly, read the Bible to her children, all of whom were baptized and tormented herself about whether it was proper to knit on the Sabbath. Although she had pledged herself never to "bother" her husband with her opinions, Darwin could not help knowing exactly how she felt about his heretical theories.

How could Darwin bring further distress to his beloved Emma, who had devoted herself to alleviating the strain and misery of his illness and shielding him from every possible annoyance? She had pampered him outrageously, raised his large family, and cheerfully maintained a home that was part workshop and laboratory.

He could remain silent. But then what of the words he had once confided to his journal: "Those who believe and yet do not openly avow their belief as much retard the progress of science as those whose false opinions they assail."

Man could not be excluded from the grand design. The book had to be written.

In *The Descent of Man* Darwin set out to show that man is descended from an animal ancestor. It was a bold task in the 1860's, since the fossil forms that link man to the other primates had not yet been discovered. Darwin was forced to rely on indirect proof.

If man is descended from earlier forms, he said, then his body should testify to "the indelible stamp of his lowly origin."

The bones, muscles, nerves, and blood vessels of man are very much like those of the other mammals. "Every chief fissure and fold in the brain of man," for example, "has its analogy in that of the orang." In other words, man is not made of brass or iron but of the very same materials as the animals. Man and the higher primates are so much alike that he can transmit his diseases to them and they to him. The poisons and drugs that affect him also affect them. The parasites that lodge in him infest them also. The human embryo at one stage possesses a vestigial tail, an indication that man is descended from ancestors that once had tails.

Man and the mammals share not only a similar body plan but also similar instincts and senses. The higher animals are capable of rage, pleasure, pain, curiosity, jealousy, and pride. They take pleasure in each other's company and perform services for each other. "One female baboon not only adopted young monkeys of other species but stole young dogs and cats. An adopted kitten scratched this affectionate baboon who certainly had a fine intellect for she immediately examined the kitten's feet and bit off the claws."

Darwin knew that the intelligence of man is vastly superior to that of the ape, but the difference is one of degree and not of kind, owing primarily to the comparative size of their brains. Yet apes are quite capable of reasoning, and not only of using crude tools but on occasion of making them. The mental gap between man and the rest of the animal kingdom is wide, but it merely indicates that man has come a long way from his original lowly state.

If man has developed from a lower form, who is his closest relative among the animals? No living animal, Darwin replied, but rather an extinct creature that was the common ancestor of both ape and man, "a hairy-tailed quadruped probably arboreal in its habits." Some of these tree-living ancestors of man, perhaps because of a change in their environment, were forced to seek life on the ground. Those able to get up on their hind limbs so that their hands were free to wield a club or a stone had the best chance of surviving and producing the greatest number of offspring. Along with the increasing ability to stand upright eventually came other bodily changes: the pelvis broadened to support the weight of the upper part of the body, the head set back on the neck, and the spine bent into an "S" curve. Thus, beginning with the hind limbs, the anatomical structure of man gradually emerged, as every favorable physical variation that helped meet the demands of the environment was encouraged by natural selection.

In *The Descent of Man* Darwin made no claim that he had demonstrated the evolution of man. Rather he indicated how man *could* have evolved, and predicted that one day the evidence would be spread before us. His prophecy is coming true.

In recent years the fossils of a number of manlike apes have come to light, for example, Kenyapithecus in Africa and a close relative, Ramapithecus, that lived in India about thirteen million years ago. The surprisingly human jaw structure and teeth of Ramapithecus offers grounds for believing that this ape was close to the stock from which the earliest men arose.

Darwin deduced that man had evolved in a series of forms graduating insensibly from the apelike to the completely human. The fossils of the australopithecines that have been found in East Africa represent a transitional stage between the nonhuman ancestors of man and later forms. Although they retained many apelike features, they were able to stand erect on quite human legs. The discovery of *Homo habilis* within the last few years in the Olduvai Gorge in Tanganyika demonstrates the existence almost two million years ago of apelike men who could build primitive shelters and make tools according to a regular pattern, although their brain capacity was not much greater than that of the gorilla or chimpanzee. *Homo habilis* may very well have been the ancestor of *Homo rectus,* a primitive man advanced enough to use fire, who in turn was almost certainly the stock from which *Homo sapiens,* or modern man, emerged.

Considering how little was known of man's ancestry in Darwin's day, it is amazing how much of *The Descent of Man* has been vindicated by discoveries in the intervening years. We may in a sense call Darwin the father of the science of anthropology, because he gave it its underlying theme, the evolution of man.

The Descent of Man, the book that thrust man out of the family of the angels and set him down among his own kin on his planet, was published on February 24, 1871.* How was the world going to receive it?

Surprisingly, public reaction was quite mild. Darwin, who had written to Hooker the month before, "The work half-killed me and I have not the most remote idea whether the book is worth publishing," could have spared himself much worry and anxiety. The kind of nastiness and ridicule that had greeted *The Origin of Species* eleven years earlier never materialized. One magazine did run a cartoon of Darwin as an apeman wielding a club in his hind limb, and the *Times* of London deplored the fact that Darwin had chosen to publish his book the very year Parliament was considering the establishment of free public schools. But, on the whole, the reaction was mild. At home even Emma took it in her stride,

---

* *The Descent of Man and Selection in Relation to Sex,* to give it its full title, is actually two studies, one on man's evolution and the other on sexual selection in the animal kingdom.

"Gorilla: 'That Man wants to claim my Pedigree. He says he is one of my Descendants.' "

"Mr. Bergh (founder of the A.S.P.C.A.): 'Now, Mr. Darwin, how could you insult him so?' "

although she could not refrain from a slight reproach: "I should dislike it for putting God farther off."

Darwin himself was amazed at how attitudes had changed. "Evolution is talked about as an accepted fact and the descent of man with calmness."

To account for Darwin's victory we must remember that

his opponents had nothing better to offer scientifically. The hypothesis of special creation was dead. No serious scientist was prepared to go back to it after Darwin's monumental demonstration in the *Origin* of the evolution of life. Some might continue to criticize and attempt to amend the principle of natural selection, but the basic structure was to survive to the present day. As early as 1865 Adam Sedgwick had already seen the handwriting on the wall: "The Geologic Society is partly in fetter. It is not the honest independent body it once was and some of its leading men are led by the nose." Translated into simple English, his remark meant that the Society once led "by the nose" by anti-evolutionists like himself was now coming over to Darwin.

By the time *The Descent of Man* appeared, "evolution" had become so respectable that the public was able to swallow the animal origin of mankind. As Lyell put it, Darwin had gone the whole *orang,* and nothing had happened!

The triumph was not Darwin's alone. Among others, Huxley and Ernst Haeckel, the German biologist, had already prepared the ground for the acceptance of *The Descent of Man* by writing about the evolution of man. Darwin had again been forestalled.

Together with respectability, Darwin acquired new and powerful champions, which was all very gratifying except that their support came when he no longer needed it. Henry Ward Beecher, the American ambassador to Britain, asserted that design by wholesale was more noble than design by retail, by which he meant that God, once He had established the laws for the government of the universe, did not intend to rescind them by individual acts of creation. God became the author of evolution, and Darwin its presiding minister.

Even the English Church eventually capitulated. Baden

Powell, the influential professor of theology at Oxford, declared that there could be no real conflict between science and religion since nature and the Bible were the work of the same divine Author, a statement echoed many times since by religious leaders. In our own time Pope Paul VI, in a speech in Pisa, Italy, praising the "great mind and immortal memory of Galileo," who had once been condemned for heresy, vigorously rejected the possibility of any contradiction between scientific truth and religion.

Thomas Huxley, who had fought so long and vigorously for Darwin, the rebel and heretic, was overjoyed with the victory of his friend. "You have the rare happiness," he wrote, "of seeing your ideas triumph in your own lifetime." And then he pretended to complain: "It is going to be a dull world. Ideas that men scorned just a quarter of a century ago will soon be taught in the textbooks. I can't stand it; I am almost prepared to go into opposition."

12

With such moderate abilities as I possess it is truly surprising that I should have influenced the belief of scientific men in some important points.

CHARLES DARWIN

The Battle Won

The battle was won, the enemy routed from the field. Darwin had dared to defy the world, and the world had surrendered. Recognition at last was his, and with it the acclaim of society. The youthful revolutionary had become the elderly sage.

With the publication of *The Descent of Man,* Darwin was able to return to his first love, field work. He was away from his desk, in the garden, woods, and greenhouse where he had always wanted to be. There were no controversies under the stones and trees. "I've taken up old botanical work and given up theories," he gaily announced.

He was fascinated by the strange behavior of the little bog plant, the common sundew (*Drosera rotundifolia*). The sundew leaf, about one-quarter of an inch across, is covered with hundreds of tiny tentacles, each ending in a gland containing sticky fluid that glitters in the sun. Let an insect become stuck in the fluid, and the tentacles at once close in on the

149

unlucky trespasser. When Darwin deposited a bit of meat in the center of one of the flowers, the tentacles enveloped it, and a juice was produced that was capable of dissolving muscle, connective tissue, cartilage, and even bone fiber. Not only could the plant capture insects; it could also absorb them into its tissues. "By Jove," Darwin cried, "I sometimes think Drosera is an animal in disguise!"

Of what advantage to Drosera was this curious adaptation that allowed it to digest and absorb flesh? To settle the question Darwin suggested to his son Frank, who was acting as his assistant at the time, that he raise two sets of Drosera, of which one set would receive a regular meat diet, and the other would not. Frank discovered that the meat-fed plants had bigger leaves, bigger seed capsules, and bigger stalks than the others. Darwin concluded that since Drosera lives in the poor soil of bogs, its ability to capture and digest insects probably is a compensation for the food elements it misses. The experiment confirmed Darwin's view that an adaptation must confer some benefit upon an organism.

Again using Frank as his assistant, Darwin now turned to a study of plant movement.* Exactly how did plants climb? Darwin knew that the growing shoot of climbing plants bends. His problem was to find out what caused the bending. He discovered that when the tip of a shoot was exposed to light, the most active growth occurred on the side away from the light and some distance down from the tip. If the tissue that was growing was sheltered from the light, growth would still take place provided only that the tip was exposed. Darwin came to the conclusion that something in the upper part of

* He summarized the results in two books: *Climbing Plants,* published in 1875, and *The Power of Movement in Plants,* published in 1880.

the plant was affected by light, and transmitted its effect to the lower part where the growth took place. This remarkable discovery opened up an important field in the study of plant physiology, and contributed to the present-day investigation of plant hormones and other growth-stimulating substances.

While Darwin toiled away in his greenhouse and garden, his health, surprisingly, began to improve. The change came just about the time he completed *The Descent of Man*. We may suspect that his improved health and the fact that he was now engaged in far less controversial work were not unconnected with each other. Drosera seems to have been a far better prescription for him than the origin of species.

Although he was much stronger, he continued to live quietly at home, revising old books, corresponding with fellow scientists, and checking on the results of his beloved experiments: a devoted, single-minded scientific worker.

Every morning, in good weather and bad, wearing a short cloak and a black slouch hat and accompanied by his white fox terrier Polly, Darwin would take his daily stroll about the Sandwalk, a one and one-half acre plot behind his house about which he had built a gravel path. In his hand he carried his trusty stick, which still bore the braided marks of the climbing plant that had once wound around it. He had a habit, as his son Frank later recalled, of counting the number of turns he did about the Sandwalk by means of "a number of flints one of which he kicked out of the path each time he passed. Sometimes when alone he stood still or walked stealthily to observe birds or beasts. On one of these occasions some young squirrels ran up his back and legs while their mother barked at them in an agony from a tree."

Indoors he often wore a short shawl. Seated in his wheelchair he scratched out the results of his observations in a hand he could not always decipher. On the side of his window he had a mirror so placed that he could see who was at the door and then decide whether he was "at home."

He lost his medals and diplomas and quite forgot to what learned societies he had been elected. Honors, degrees, tributes, and requests for his portrait meant far less to him than the crawling life he found under a stone in his meadow.

In 1877, Cambridge finally got around to honoring her most distinguished son, and Darwin, who had steadfastly ignored both the world's acclaim and its contempt, agreed, to everyone's surprise, to appear for the occasion. The undergraduates, jammed in the aisles and perched on the statues and window ledges, good-naturedly yelled and catcalled. Roars of laughter greeted the appearance of a toy monkey that dangled from a cord stretched between the balconies. Suddenly there was a hush followed by an outburst of cheering. The doors opened, and Darwin emerged dressed in a red robe. Preceded by a squadron of brightly clad dons, he walked slowly and serenely to the platform. The Public Orator made a long speech. The Vice-Chancellor in his scarlet and white robes murmured a few Latin words over the bent, shaggy-browed, bright-eyed old man, bestowing on him the honorary degree of Bachelor of Laws. The uncertain, reluctant student who had left his university forty-seven years ago had graciously returned to accept its homage.

That evening Cambridge held a great public dinner for Darwin. But the excitement had been too much for him, and he spent the evening with Emma as his only company. Speaking for the absent hero, Huxley rose to offer Darwin's thanks, but then, unable to restrain himself, caustically assailed the university for having withheld its recognition until the battle had been won and all risk past.

Down House in Kent—and study—where Darwin lived
from 1842 until his death.

One morning in 1879 Darwin came down to London and dropped in unexpectedly on Huxley's class at the Royal College of Science. One of the students, Henry Fairfield Osborn, later to become president of the American Museum of Natural History in New York, remembered the occasion all his life. "He stands much taller than Huxley," wrote Osborn, "has a very ruddy face with benevolent blue eyes and overhanging brows. His face is quite long and perfectly white and his hair falls partly over a low forehead. His features are not good. My general impression of his face is very pleasant."

Huxley brought Darwin over to meet the startled Osborn. "I gave Darwin's hand a tremendous squeeze and said in almost a reverential tone, 'I am so glad to see you.' Huxley then hurried him into the next room saying, 'I must not let you talk too much.' The instant Huxley closed the door I was mobbed as the lucky American by the ninety less fortunate students."

Darwin never quite comprehended how he had become one of the great men of his time. The reverence Osborn and others felt toward him he would have found quite puzzling. How had he, Charles Darwin, ever become a serious student? How had he ever written a book worthy of publication? How had he ever given birth to a serious scientific idea? Like a poverty-stricken child overwhelmed by unexpected toys, he never ceased being astonished by the honors that accumulated about him. "With such modest abilities as I possess it is surprising that I should have influenced the belief of scientific men on some important points. . . . I have often regretted that I did not do more direct good for my fellow men." Over the recognition, the acclaim, and the prizes still hovered the shadow of his early lack of confidence.

A severe self-critic, seemingly afraid that if he didn't tear at himself someone else would, he was overcome by his mistakes. Once, when an investigation had gone wrong and he realized that several weeks of work had been wasted, he cried out in bleak despair, "I am the most miserable befuddled stupid dog in all England!" *Dog!* It was not the only time the image rose in his mind when he thought of himself. The portraits of his last years reveal him as a trim, ascetic, awe-inspiring figure, and yet looking at one of them he could say, "I look a very venerable melancholy old dog." Never did a great man, hailed and admired in his own age, entertain more self-doubt.

His father's influence showed up in strange ways. The boy who had so often been reprimanded for extravagance grew up to practice absurd economies. To save writing paper he wrote within the margins and over the backs of manuscripts and old letters. He deemed it an extravagance to buy a book that could be obtained from a friend or the public library. He could not even discard a bit of twisted paper with which he had lighted a candle, but must use it a second time.

He dreaded poverty so much that the feeling passed on to his children. His son Frank remembered his saying with great solemnity, "Thank God, you will always have bread and cheese." At the time the boy interpreted the remark to mean that bread and cheese was about all he ever would have.

And yet Charles Darwin was a wealthy man. Childlike and unworldly in some ways, he was nevertheless a shrewd investor, increasing his father's inheritance, plus the profits from his own books, to a sizable fortune that at his death came to £282,000. Today it would amount to something approaching $2,000,000. Remarkably exact in business matters, he kept his accounts with great care, classifying and balancing them as though he were running a mercantile establishment. Emma,

Darwin in his last years. "What I shall do with my few remaining years I can hardly tell. I have everything to make me happy and contented but life has become very wearisome to me."

catching the habit, kept her own record of household bills, donations to charity, and even cab fares, though she could never hope to achieve her husband's degree of exactness.

Money had a way of seeking Darwin out. In 1878, he received a letter from a complete stranger named Anthony Rich who announced that he was going to leave a large property to Darwin at his death. Darwin pleaded that he was already a wealthy man, and needed nothing. Rich, however, was insistent: Darwin must become his heir. Two years later, when Darwin inherited a good part of his brother Erasmus's fortune, he again protested to his benefactor, but Rich was adamant. In the end, however, Rich failed to achieve his wish, for he lived until 1891, and by that time Darwin had already been dead for nine years.

As Darwin became older, he drew closer to his father. A short time before the death of Dr. Darwin, Charles went up to Shrewsbury to visit him. The two sick men, father and son, sat side by side in the garden of the great red-brick house. The lotus tree Charles had brought back from his *Beagle* voyage and planted in a corner of the garden was now several stories high. Looking down into the valley, Charles could see the river Severn winding about the town and the spires of his old school rising above the housetops.

Charles must have felt a vast sympathy for the infirm old man who in his own way had tried to be good to him. Robert Darwin may have been harsh and tyrannical toward his children, but what he was and the way he behaved were in part the result of his own upbringing. As a boy he also had been overshadowed by a domineering father. Like Charles, he had never wanted to become a physician. Like Charles, he had dreaded the sight of blood. Unlike Charles, however, he had never dared to go counter to *his* father's wishes.

Charles Darwin possibly could have avoided a lifetime of suffering by yielding to what his father and society demanded of him. At every step along the way he had to make a choice between conformity and being true to himself. How easy to have become a physician and inherited his father's lucrative and respected practice! How easy to have been a country parson indulging his little hobbies and going off bird hunting! How easy to have entered an academic career at the university and repeated and embellished the lessons Sedgwick and Henslow had taught him! In the end, however, the shy, affectionate son turned out to be far tougher than the inflexible father.

Any bitterness Charles may have felt toward his father fled with the passing years. Whatever resentment there had been in the past was either made light of or forgotten. "My father was a little unjust to me when I was young," he wrote, "but afterward I am thankful to think I became a prime favorite with him."

In 1880, Darwin approached his publisher, John Murray, and apologetically asked him to accept what proved to be his last book. "Here is a work that has absorbed me for many years. I fear the subject will not interest the public, but will you publish it for me?"

"What is the subject?" asked Murray.

"Earthworms," Darwin replied.

Darwin's uncle, Josiah Wedgwood, had once suggested to him that earthworms undermined anything resting on the surface by bringing up soil. In his new book, *Formation of Vegetable Mould through the Action of Worms,* published in 1881, Darwin attempted a precise study of the effect these small creatures have on the soil. He studied their habits, their anatomy, and even their reaction to sound. When his son Frank played his bassoon for them, they did not respond, but when they were placed on the piano and a bass note was struck, they immediately became disturbed. They were probably reacting, Darwin reasoned, to the vibrations rather than to the sound. He had an almost childlike eagerness to try out the most improbable ideas, though others might consider them a waste of time. "Fools' experiments," he called them.

To determine the rate at which objects sank into the ground, he constructed a "wormstone" on his own lawn, a flat rock to which he attached a measuring scale. He calculated that earthworms "sank" the stone at the rate of one-quarter of an inch a year.

At Stonehenge, Darwin inspected the vast ring of monumental stones that had been erected by a mysterious people in the dim past. Many of them were overturned and embedded in the earth. Darwin demonstrated that their submergence had been caused by earthworms that had been burrowing under them for many centuries.

Far more significant for man than the earthworm's role in burying old monuments was the part it played in enriching the soil. An earthworm eats decayed vegetation and conveys it to its humus-lined burrow. Then it swallows earth, grinds it to a powder, and brings it up to the surface, where it is discarded as worm castings. Thus it continuously moves, tills, and enriches the earth.

The book had an unusually good sale for such a topic. "In the eyes of most men," wrote one reviewer, "the earthworm is a mere dumb senseless and unpleasantly slimy animal. Mr. Darwin undertakes to rehabilitate his character and he now steps forward as an intelligent and beneficent personage, a worker of great geological change."

What had aroused Darwin's interest in the earthworm was not its supposed intelligence but its ability to bring about geological change. Exerting an infinitely minute effort, it had gradually helped to alter the earth's surface. It seemed as if

To determine the rate at which earthworms undermine surface structures, Darwin built the "wormstone" on his lawn at Down.

this "dumb senseless and unpleasantly slimy animal" had been reading Lyell.

The earthworm book brought Darwin back full circle to his first significant observation on the *Beagle* voyage fifty years ago. The great transformations of the earth have not been the result of overwhelming catastrophe, but the cumulative effect of small slow changes over vast periods of time. Like the rest of Darwin's gigantic contribution to human knowledge, the modest little earthworm study turned out to be a vindication of the principle of Uniformitarianism.

By 1881, Darwin appeared to be in such good health that he was able to travel about more frequently. In the late autumn he went down to London to visit his daughter Henrietta. On December 13th he went to see a friend, Mr. G. J. Romanes, and experienced his first heart attack. Mr. Romanes happened to be out, and the servant immediately offered to get him a cab. It was typical of Darwin to avoid giving others trouble, and despite his distress he insisted upon finding one for himself.

That winter the attacks increased in frequency. On March 7th, while attempting to walk about his meadow, he became seriously ill. Then on the early morning of Wednesday, April 19, 1882, he called Emma to his side. He thanked her and the children for having been so good to him, and apologized for having caused them any distress. "I am not the least afraid to die," he said. He died that afternoon at the age of seventy-three, living his last moments as he had lived his life, calmly, courageously, modestly.

Darwin had hoped to be buried next to his brother in the village churchyard at Downe about a mile from his home. But a few days after his death a petition was circulated in

Parliament requesting his burial in Westminster Abbey, the final resting-place of so many of Britain's famous men. That the request was promptly granted indicates how far Darwin had come toward universal acceptance and respectability.

In his death the outcast who had shocked the entire Victorian world received the solemn tribute of Church and State. Nobility and commoners alike came to the services, representatives of foreign nations and famous universities, prominent figures from every walk of life. Darwin's beloved widow alone did not attend. Emma, who had so often kept her retiring husband company at home, now chose to mourn in the seclusion of Down. Her eldest son, William, went in her place, and by his presence added a Darwinian footnote to the solemn proceedings. While the entire company sat in bareheaded respect in the great Cathedral, William, who had been warned by his doting father ever to beware of drafts, kept his bald head covered with his black gloves throughout the service.

Among the pallbearers were Alfred Wallace, the co-discoverer of natural selection; Joseph Hooker, Darwin's faithful comrade and fellow worker; and Thomas Huxley, the best and sturdiest of champions. Charles Lyell, of whom Darwin had said, "I always felt as if my books came half out of Lyell's brain," had died several years before.

Darwin's grave in Westminster Abbey, over which the visitor may unwittingly walk without seeing it, is close to the choir screen in the north aisle of the nave, a few feet from that of Sir Isaac Newton. The worn gray stone bears the simplest of inscriptions:

CHARLES ROBERT DARWIN
BORN 12 FEBRUARY 1809
DIED 19 APRIL 1882

13

Long before the reader will have arrived at this part of my book [The Origin of Species] *a crowd of difficulties will have occurred to him. Some are so serious that to this day I can hardly reflect on them without being to some degree staggered.*

CHARLES DARWIN

Darwin Today

In the principle of natural selection Darwin gave mankind the grandest and most comprehensive hypothesis in the history of science since Newton's formulation of the universal laws of gravitation. Impersonal and objective, natural selection presents a satisfactory explanation of a vast number of events in living nature in the simplest and most economical way. In the more than one hundred years since the publication of *The Origin of Species,* no one has seriously challenged it.

And yet there is a gap in the principle, a weakness that Darwin himself was the first to acknowledge. Evolution can occur only because all organisms differ among themselves. Even two barnacles, Darwin discovered, are not exactly alike. Were all individuals identical, evolution would have no place in the scheme of things. Species change because natural selection preserves some differences and eliminates others. Without variation in plants and animals, there obviously would be nothing to select from.

Natural selection, however, cannot account for the origin of differences. How do variations arise? * How are they inherited? "What the devil determines each particular variation?" Darwin wrote to Huxley. "What makes a tuft of feathers come on a cock's head or moss on a moss rose?" All that Darwin could say in answer to his own questions was that "the laws governing inheritance are quite unknown."

Actually, the key to the puzzle was found in 1866, only seven years after the appearance of the *Origin*. In that year an obscure Czechoslovakian monk, Gregor Mendel, published a paper that aroused so little attention that neither Darwin nor the rest of the scientific community knew anything about it. Experimenting with the ordinary garden pea in his monastery garden in Brno, Mendel had worked out the basic formulation of the laws of inheritance. Then in the year 1900 not one but three researchers, Hugo De Vries in Amsterdam, Karl Correns in Tübingen, and Erich Tschermak von Seysenegg in Vienna rediscovered Mendel's laws, each knowing nothing of the other's work or of Mendel's pioneering discoveries.

The reason Mendel's discovery was overlooked so long may be that he unfortunately selected for some of his follow-up experiments an unsuitable plant, the hawkweed, one of the few organisms in the whole of the plant and animal kingdoms with which it is most difficult to demonstrate the laws of inheritance. Since he could not confirm his garden-pea findings with his hawkweed experiments, Mendel may have been discouraged from bringing his work to the attention of other

---

* That is, variations that are inherited, passing from generation to generation. Variations or modifications caused by differences in the environment, such as climate, altitude, or food supply are not inherited and play no part in evolution.

botanists. His failure to achieve public recognition in his own lifetime is one of the great tragedies of science.

Today we know that the physical basis of inheritance is located in the chromosomes within the nuclei of plant and animal cells. Within each chromosome, arranged in pairs in a definite order, are large chemical molecules called genes. Individual genes are associated with the characteristics we inherit from our parents: eye color, height, shape of nose, blood group, hairiness, and so on. A particular gene may control certain characteristics, but this control is influenced by all the other genes. Acting together, the genes constitute a gene complex, a kind of balanced team in which each gene affects and is affected by all the others.

We may think of the genes as packets of information that direct the heredity of the offspring. Children are like their parents because they have inherited their genetic code.

Yet offspring do differ from their parents. How do variations arise?

Genes are stable structures that remain constant for long periods. On infrequent occasions, however, for reasons that are not quite understood, a mutation, or change, will take place in one of them, with the result that the offspring will differ from its parents. (Mutation is supposed to be a change in the chemical structure in the nucleoprotein of the chromosome.) The gene then in its changed state is passed on to future generations. Some mutations have such an overwhelming effect that the offspring either fails to develop or, having been born, does not live to maturity.

As the result of mutations in past generations, the genetic outfit of each individual contains countless pairs of dissimilar genes. In the process of inheritance the genes are reassembled and recombined. The possible number of combinations is enormous. Such recombinations bring about gradual and continuous changes in all forms of life on earth.

Today, then, we have the solution to the question that puzzled Darwin so much. Variations arise as the result of gene recombination and the spontaneous mutation of individual genes. There is already so much variation in plants and animals that were mutation to come to an end now, evolution would continue for as long a period into the future as it has gone on up to the present.

Environment, also, has a role to play. Between the environment and the genes that determine heredity there exists a highly complex relationship. One might suppose that certain body structures, a pair of eyes, for example, are guaranteed, as it were, by the laws of inheritance. After all, vertebrate animals have been passing this paired arrangement on to each other for over 400 million years. Yet if a fish embryo is permitted to develop in water containing a salt such as magnesium chloride, it matures as a cyclops, a single-eyed creature.

It seems that genes cannot produce normal individuals unless the environmental factors are also normal. Strictly speaking, then, we do not inherit the characteristics with which we are born. "What is inherited," says Sir Gavin de Beer, former director of the Natural History section of the British Museum, "is a packet of genes transmitted from the parents with the capacity to respond to environmental conditions in certain ways, some of which are called normal for the species in its normal environment. . . ."

We may look at inheritance through two windows, the Darwinian and the genetic, and discover that we are looking at the same scene. As Darwin saw it, variations arose from unknown causes. When variations produced disadvantages, they were eventually eliminated by natural selection. When they conferred advantages, they became capable of further improvement, again by means of natural selection. Thus, given sufficient time, evolutionary changes could take place.

As the modern student of genetics sees the picture, variations are caused by gene mutation and gene recombination. Once variations arise, natural selection takes over. Disadvantageous variations are suppressed, and beneficial variations are preserved and improved. Modern genetics has not changed the basic ground rules of the evolutionary game.

There are a number of exceptional cases, however, where a disadvantageous gene may confer a benefit on its possessors. For example, in areas of Central Africa where malaria is prevalent there is a serious inherited disease called sickle-cell anemia. The gene that carries this disease has become established because it is linked to a beneficial trait: those who carry it are resistant to the malaria parasite. In regions where malaria is rampant, therefore, it may be of some advantage to possess the sickle-cell gene. We might say that natural selection has made the best of a bad gene complex.

The general rule is that a mutation is not going to spread widely if natural selection is operating against it. For example, a mutant gene that gives moths a conspicuous color probably will not flourish, since the insects that carry it fall easy prey to birds, and are soon killed off.

Until a century ago the English peppered moth was protected by its gray color, which matched the tree trunk on which it rested during the day. On occasion a black mutant strain would show up in the population. The principle of natural selection suggests that the gray moths would be favored by their inconspicuous color and that the blacks would never become firmly established, and this is exactly what happened. The black mutants were so rare that they were prized as collectors' items.

But then modern industry came and altered the environment. Within the last few decades factory smoke has blackened the trunks of the trees on which the peppered moths rest. The formerly inconspicuous grays have now become conspicuous, fallen victim to birds, and decreased rapidly in number. The scarce blacks merged with their sooty background and increased in number. A century ago the dark variety formed less than 1 percent of the moth population; today in industrial areas it forms 99 percent. The gray moth is now the variety.

"The peppered moth," says Professor de Beer, "has evolved from grey to black. The black has become intensified. The change was brought about by natural selection of a variety due to mutation, and this little piece of evolution has taken place in one hundred years under the observation of man."

The evolution of the English peppered moth demonstrates that the laws of genetics and the principle of natural selection do not conflict with but rather complement each other. While gene mutation and gene recombination produce the variations that are the raw materials of change, natural selection, the force behind evolution, determines the rate and direction of change. The modern formulation of natural selection differs a little from Darwin's. Whereas Darwin stressed the key role of the struggle for existence, modern theory places the emphasis on what is called "differential reproduction." Those organisms are favored that produce the most offspring. In most cases this means those best adapted to the conditions under which they live.

Not all Darwin's ideas have been confirmed by later investigation. New knowledge, new techniques, and new equipment inevitably lead to the modification of the conclusions of the greatest scientists. We do not criticize Newton for having failed to anticipate the Einsteinian concept of relativity. What is so amazing about Darwin is that in the century since the publication of *The Origin of Species,* despite all the advances that have been made in the biological sciences, we have had so little occasion to modify his basic discoveries.

Today the burning issue, as Julian Huxley has said, is no longer the origin of species but the origin of life itself.* It was natural that the problem should puzzle Darwin as it puzzles us.

He saw no need for the miraculous intervention of a super-being to get life started, just as he saw no necessity of special creation to account for the origin of species. If life could evolve in accord with the laws of nature, it could also originate under the same authority. "If it is ever found that life can originate in this world," he wrote, "the vital phenomena will come under some general law of nature."

His suggestion was that a combination of ammonia and phosphoric salts in the presence of light, heat, and electricity could be transformed into protein compounds that in the course of time might evolve into the very first form of life on this globe.

In this remarkable speculation Darwin anticipated some of the contemporary investigations of life's beginning. In 1952, at the suggestion of the atomic physicist Dr. Harold Urey, the American biologist S. L. Miller passed ultraviolet light and strong electrical discharges through a mixture of water, methane, hydrogen, and ammonia. He discovered that he had created amino acids, the building blocks of the protein molecule.

---

* One of the strangest theories about the origin of life was that of the Greek philosopher Empedocles, who, in the fifth century B.C. suggested that in the beginning there were various body parts, limbs, heads, and trunks, knocking about loose. These came together by chance, and of the many combinations that were produced only the workable ones survived.

On the strength of Miller's pioneering experiment, we may imagine that the first proteins were created in the warm salt-water ponds of our planet about three billion years ago in somewhat the same way. Since no protective layer of ozone blanketed the earth, ultraviolet radiation from the sun could reach mixtures of inorganic compounds in the water and provide the energy for the necessary chemical change. Once the new organic compounds achieved the proper degree of concentration, some of them built a membrane around others and formed the first primitive living cells. Probably many hundreds of millions of years went by before any of them achieved anything resembling the complexity of bacteria and protozoa.

Some of the new organisms eventually became plants, synthesizing their own body tissue out of simpler materials through the action of sunlight working on chlorophyll or some other colored substance. Others became animals, obtaining their food supply by devouring the plants.

Could life arise spontaneously today? Probably not. The physical and chemical conditions that prevailed three billion years ago do not exist at the present time, and therefore we cannot expect that life could arise in the same way. When life is again created on this planet, it will undoubtedly be in the laboratory.

Whatever the details of the origin of life, we can feel certain that it evolved out of nonliving matter—unless we are to believe that it was brought here from outer space. All our current inquiries tend to confirm the validity of Darwin's thinking.

In our own time Darwin's influence has spread far beyond his speculations and discoveries. Virtually every aspect of human thought has felt the impact of his work.

In the same way that the great astronomers of the seventeenth century revolutionized man's way of thinking about the universe, Darwin in the nineteenth century altered man's way of thinking about living things. In the Middle Ages men had imagined that the stars and the planets were set in a series of concentric shells that were kept in continuous motion by God and His angels. But Kepler, Galileo, and Newton showed that the heavens were self-propelled, and moved in conformity to impersonal laws.

The generation that saw the publication of *The Origin of Species* was able to accept science's dominion over stars and planets but could not forego God's custody over trees, beetles, turtles, barnacles, and man. Darwin was vehemently denounced as the most dangerous man in England simply because he denied the judgment of the clergy in the plant and animal kingdoms. Life was a sacred preserve immune to the encroachments of the natural order of the inorganic world.

But Darwin insisted that the authority of science applied to the living world with as much force as it did to the inorganic. At the heart of life was not a supernatural mystery but a universal rule subject to scientific inquiry and experimentation. The laws of nature had their origin not from without but from within nature itself.

Once Western man learned to accept evolution as a universal principle, he discovered that the door had been flung wide open to the scientific investigation of almost every human activity. There were no longer any tabooed topics. All aspects of living—society, right and wrong, sex, the innermost processes of the mind—became subject to the rigors of scientific examination. In a way the work of Freud would have been unthinkable without that of Darwin.

Darwin shattered for all time the illusions that had given strength and hope to countless generations. Man was no longer a privileged being specially created and enthroned above all other forms of life. He was only one example of the many variations nature can improvise on the theme of life. His history began not in heaven but on the surface of this planet; his early story was identical with that of the fish, the lizards, the toads, and the nonhuman primates. "Your beginning," we may imagine Darwin saying, "was lowly, your destiny uncertain. You are not the highest creature evolution can produce, and probably not the last. Your continued residence on this earth depends on your ability to adapt to changing ways of life, including the transformations Science is effecting every day. You too can become as extinct as the Megatherium or Toxodon whose bleached bones I once long ago found strewn on the red sands of Patagonia."

In destroying the ancient myths, however, Darwin also instilled a great hope in us. We are not angels but are made of the same substance as all other life. And if we are not angels we are not fallen creatures, but beings upon whom the evolutionary process has bestowed the power of reason. What faults we have are ours alone, and not of our stars. We alone of all organisms that dwell on earth have understanding. If our problems are made by man, they can also be solved by man.

Behind the revolution Darwin wrought in human affairs, behind the scientific discoveries, behind the countless experiments and observations, looms the man. What was Darwin's special genius?

For one who became a brilliant and tireless scholar, he began as a miserable failure. Were he applying to one of our great universities today, he almost certainly would be turned down:

Candidate apathetic without direction. Special interests: bird shooting and beetle collecting. Secondary school record very poor. Usual letter of regret.

Darwin was a slow starter, and all of us who are late bloomers can take comfort in his later career. Shrewsbury Grammar School, the scene of his early academic defeats, today proudly preserves the doodles he once scrawled across the pages of his textbook.

He was, as he described himself, "a millionaire in odd and curious facts," but these facts and the conclusions that he extracted from them made no immediate impression on his fellow scientists. They saw nature as a kind of scattered jigsaw puzzle, the pieces of which were not intended to fit together, animals and plants separately created and unrelated. But Darwin conceived of nature as a totality of interrelating and interlocking organisms branching out from each other and then flowing out to occupy all the empty niches on the planet.

Darwin was not the first to see nature as a unity or evolution as the pattern that gave it meaning. But the work of his predecessors was developed casually, and could never have withstood the test of rigorous scientific proof. Evolution had no reality until he identified the agency by which it operates: natural selection.

There was little that did not arouse his curiosity. The enormous collection he brought back to England from his five-year voyage provides a long catalogue of his interests: minerals, plants, insects, spiders, shellfish, teeth and bones of animals living and dead. When he arrived home, experts in the natural sciences gaped at the richness and extent of what he had gathered and vied for the privilege of cataloguing his treasures. "I think," he once wrote with characteristic understatement, "I am superior to the common run of men in noticing things which easily escape attention."

He also noticed things that lay buried deep beneath the surface. He saw history in a blade of grass. Just as Lyell looked upon a mountain and envisioned the thousands of small events that had built it, Darwin looked upon the adaptation of an orchid that ensures cross-fertilization, and saw the untold number of variations that led step by step to the final structure. No living thing had sprung into existence as if by command. All organisms were the result of centuries of change and development. Thanks, in good part, to Darwin, biology acquired a new dimension: time.

Darwin had the rare ability to look out upon the world as though he were the very first one to do so. He was not apt, as he said, to follow blindly the lead of other men. He was able not only to reject the theories by which his generation explained nature but also to go further and to entertain ideas that responsible scholars considered downright foolish and even heretical. We may marvel that intelligent and educated men were willing to accept as fact the ancient fables about the origin of species current at the time. But we must remember that such tales were closely linked to religious faith. Woe to him who dared challenge them. Such a man would have to possess a stubborn conviction in the correctness of his views, a vast capacity for absorbing criticism and calumny, and a willingness to wait patiently until the world was ready to put aside passion and prejudice and weigh the evidence objectively.

There was one further quality that Darwin possessed: a passion not merely for collecting facts but also for explaining them. From his earliest youth, he recalled, he had had the strongest desire to understand what he observed by grouping the facts under some general law. On his walking tour of North Wales he had been astonished at Sedgwick for considering the presence of a tropical shell in England as an isolated fact. Charles wanted to know what conclusions could be drawn from such an extraordinary find.

The similarities as well as the differences among animals and plants that Darwin observed on the *Beagle* voyage cried out for an explanation. There had to be a unifying theme that accounted for the phenomena of life, much as Newton's principle of gravitation explained the movement of the heavenly bodies. Darwin discovered his general law in the principle of natural selection, and then, in the most comprehensive research any man had attempted in his generation in the field of natural science, he provided the documentation for it. "There is nothing comparable," as Thomas Huxley said, "to *The Origin of Species* as a connected survey of the phenomena of life permeated and vivified by a central idea."

Darwin once summed up his own qualities as a scientist: "I think I have become a little more skilful in guessing right explanations and in devising experimental tests. . . . My success as a man of science has been determined . . . by a love of science, unbounded patience in long reflecting over any subject, industry in observing and collecting facts and a fair share of invention and common sense." And then he adds this very human note: "This pure love, however, has been much aided by the ambition to be esteemed by my fellow naturalists."

NOTE

The dialogue throughout the book is based on letters Darwin and his contemporaries wrote to one another, Darwin's own published work, and reports of actual conversations. Where no other source is indicated, the quotations in the three chapters "The Voyage of the *Beagle*," "The High Andes," and "The Galápagos Islands" are from *The Voyage of H.M.S. 'Beagle.'* In the chapter " 'Shooting, Dogs, and Rat-catching,' " in which several events from Darwin's childhood have been juxtaposed, the author has attempted to reconstruct the young boy's thoughts and feelings from memories Darwin recorded many years later in his autobiography and from the most useful *Annals of Shrewsbury School* by G. W. Fisher.

Further Reading on Darwin

In the list of Darwin's principal works the date of original publication is given in parentheses after the title. The lists of books about Darwin and books about evolution in general are not definitive but include titles of particular interest.

DARWIN'S PRINCIPAL WORKS

The Descent of Man, and Selection in Relation to Sex (1871). New York: D. Appleton & Company, 1930.

Effects of Cross and Self-Fertilisation in the Vegetable Kingdom (1876). New York: D. Appleton & Company, 1895.

The Expression of the Emotions in Man and Animals (1872). Chicago: University of Chicago Press, 1965.

The Formation of Vegetable Mould, through the Action of Worms, with Observations on Their Habits (1881). New York: D. Appleton & Company, 1882.

Geological Observations on the Volcanic Islands and Parts of South America Visited during the Voyage of H.M.S. 'Beagle' (1846). New York: D. Appleton & Company, 1896.

Insectivorous Plants (1875). New York: D. Appleton & Company, 1889.

Journal of Researches into the Natural History and Geology of the Countries Visited during the Voyage of H.M.S. 'Beagle' round the World, under the Command of Capt. Fitz Roy, R.N. (1839). New York: D. Appleton & Company, 1897.

On the Movements and Habits of Climbing Plants (1865). New York: D. Appleton & Company, 1876.

On the Origin of Species by means of Natural Selection, or the Preservation of Favoured Races in the Struggle for Life (1859). New York: D. Appleton & Company, 1876.

On the Various Contrivances by Which British and Foreign Orchids Are Fertilised by Insects (1862). New York: D. Appleton & Company, 1892.

The Power of Movement in Plants (1880). Assisted by Frances Darwin. New York: D. Appleton & Company, 1881.

The Structure and Distribution of Coral Reefs (1842). Berkeley: University of California Press, 1962.

The Variation of Animals and Plants under Domestication (1868). New York: D. Appleton & Company, 193?.

Books About Darwin

Apes, Angels and Victorians by William Irvine. New York: Meridian Books, 1955.

Autobiography and Selected Letters, Edited by Frances Darwin. New York: Dover Publications, Inc., 1958.

Charles Darwin by Gavin de Beer. New York: Doubleday, 1964.

Charles Darwin and His World by Julian S. Huxley and H. B. D. Kettlewell. New York: Viking, 1965.

Darwin's Biological Work, Edited by Peter R. Bell. London: Cambridge University Press, 1959.

Background Reading

The Antecedents of Man by W. E. LeGros Clark. New York: Torchbooks, 1963.

The Evolution of Man by G. H. R. von Koenigswald. Ann Arbor: Ann Arbor Books, 1962.

A Handbook on Evolution by Gavin de Beer. London: British Museum, 1959.

History of the Primates by W. E. LeGros Clark. Chicago: University of Chicago Press, 1960.

Mankind Evolving by Theodosius Dobzhansky. New Haven: Yale University Press, 1962.

The Meaning of Evolution by G. G. Simpson. New Haven: Yale University Press, 1960.

Glossary

Adaptations: conspicuous structures or behavior patterns that enable the organism to thrive in its particular environment and leave fertile offspring. For example, the size, shape, and color of insects are adaptations that enable them to escape their enemies by merging with their backgrounds.

Anthropology: the science of man. Its several branches include physical anthropology, the evolution of man and his physical characteristics; cultural anthropology, man's ways of living; archaeology, prehistoric and extinct cultures; ethnology, the living cultures of mankind, especially of primitive peoples; and linguistics, the languages of man.

Artificial selection: the deliberate breeding of plants and animals to produce the traits the breeder is seeking. Darwin's observation of the effects of selection in breeding domestic plants and animals led him to search for a "natural" selection among plants and animals in nature.

Barnacles: crustaceans (shellfish) of the order Cirripedia, many of which cling to timbers, rocks, and the bottoms of ships.

Biology: the science of living things, including several subdivisions —botany, the study of plants; zoology, the study of animals; and ecology, the study of the relations between the organism and its environment. Darwin's earthworm book was a pioneering study in ecology.

Catastrophism: the doctrine that catastrophes similar to the Biblical flood had repeatedly destroyed life in the past and that after each such universal disaster, life was again produced through new acts of creation.

Chromosomes: small bodies within the nuclei of the cells of plants and animals that carry the genes. The number and type of the chromosomes are constant for each species.

178

Classification (taxonomy): the arrangement of animals and plants into groups based on resemblance. Grouping within larger groups reflects the course of evolution, the result of descent from common ancestors. All living men, for example, are members of one group, the species *Homo sapiens,* which is part of the family of the hominoids, a group that also includes the apes. The hominoid family belongs within the suborder of the anthropoids, which contains monkeys, apes, and men. This suborder is a part of the larger order of the primates, within which are found the tree shrews, lemurs, tarsiers, monkeys, apes, and men.

Embryology: the study of the origin of the individual organism and its development in its earliest stages, such as before its emergence from the egg.

Evolution: the process of biological change that has modified the simplest forms of life into enormously complex and varied organisms. The selective pressures of the environment on genetic variation (natural selection) is responsible for the direction and speed of evolution.

Fertilization: the union of male and female reproductive cells to form a new organism.

Fossils: traces, impressions, and remains of animals and plants of an earlier age, such as leaf- or foot-prints, bone, shell, horn, or wood.

Gene: the chemical unit of inheritance, made up principally of DNA, or deoxyribonucleic acid, located in the chromosomes.

Immutability of species: the doctrine commonly held prior to Darwin that species once created were not subject to change, each species emerging from the hand of the creator very much as it appears in the present. In its extreme form the doctrine held that man himself had originated as a civilized human being, though some men may have slipped into barbarism and savagery from their original noble state.

Monolith: a block of stone of considerable size, like those of Stonehenge.

Mutation: a change that takes place from time to time in the genes, and therefore involving a change in the traits they control. Evolution most commonly occurs on the basis of the natural selection of small mutations.

Natural selection: the agency that determines the speed and direction of evolution. Darwin observed that since individuals vary, some are more likely to succeed than others in the struggle for existence. The parents of the next generation will be selected from among the individuals that possess those variations that make for effective adaptation to the environment. Changes will gradually take place as each generation improves on the degree of adaptation realized by its ancestors. Students of evolution today see natural selection in terms of differential reproduction. Through natural selection unfavorable mutations are eliminated and favorable mutations are spread through the population.

Neanderthal man: a variety of man widely scattered through the earth that lived from about 150,000 to 50,000 years ago. The reasons for his disappearance are not known, though it is likely that he merged with the rest of the human population through interbreeding.

Physiology: the science concerned with the function of living organisms, whether plant or animal.

Protoplasm: the physical basis of life; the living matter of all animal and vegetable cells possessing the ability to grow and reproduce.

Revelation: God's communication to mankind of His existence and His will.

Sexual selection: a theory of Darwin's to explain the origin of striking colors, behavior patterns, and structures found only in one sex; for example, the remarkable tail feathers of the male lyrebird. Individuals with such characteristics, according to Darwin, had greater breeding success, and hence produced more offspring.

Special creation: the view held until Darwin's day that each species had been separately created in the beginning and had not changed.

Species: a group of animals or plants with strong resemblances to one another. Individual members normally breed only within the group.

Struggle for existence: the competition for survival in nature. Actual battle among competing individuals plays only a minor part in the struggle. Survival more often depends on ability to rear the young, tolerance of extremes of temperature, and cooperation. The swarming of insects, the herding of quadrupeds, the schooling of fish, all of which are activities not usually associated with struggle, have also played a role in survival.

Trypanosome: a minute protozoan parasite found in the blood or tissues of vertebrate animals, including man. *Trypanosoma cruzi* is the trypanosome that causes Chagas' disease, the illness that may have been the cause of Darwin's invalidism.

Uniformitarianism: the doctrine developed by James Hutton in 1785 and Charles Lyell in 1830 that geological causes operating in the present could with sufficient time have been responsible for all the past events in the development of the earth.

Variations: inheritable differences among the members of a species, such as those of size, strength, fertility, longevity, and countless other characteristics. Darwin noted that under the intense competition of life those variations would be preserved that helped the organism to leave fertile offspring and that those would eventually be eliminated that decreased its capacity to do so.

Varieties: groups within a species distinguished by inherited differences not great enough to prevent crossbreeding. According to Darwin, a species begins as a variety of an old one, and by descent and modification eventually evolves into a new species. Species are not immutable, but have sprung from varieties of other species.

A Darwin Calendar

1827-1831: attends Cambridge University ("I got into a sporting set including some low-minded dissipated young men.")

1831, December 27: sails on H.M.S. *Beagle* ("I had run a very serious risk of being rejected because of the shape of my nose.")

> *1832: First Reform Bill in England*

1832: travels in Brazil ("I first saw a tropical forest in all its sublime grandeur.")

> *1834: McCormack reaper is patented*

1834: travels in Chile ("I have thoroughly enjoyed scrambling about these huge mountains.")

1835: lands in Galápagos Islands ("The most remarkable feature of this archipelago is that different islands are inhabited by a different set of beings.")

> *1836: First telegraph lines are opened*

1836: returns to England ("I often have the most vivid and delightful pictures of what I saw on board the *Beagle* pass before my eyes. I would not change these recollections for twice ten-thousand a year.")

> *1837: Victoria becomes Queen of England*

1837: begins his first notebook on evolution; develops first symptoms of illness ("I have not been well of late.")

1838: reads "Essay on the Principle of Population" by Thomas Malthus ("I happened to read for amusement Malthus on Population . . . and it at once struck me that favorable variations would tend to be preserved and unfavorable ones destroyed.")

> *1839: Daguerreotype comes into use*

1839: marries Emma Wedgwood; first child is born ("I had not the smallest conception there was so much in a five-month baby.")

1842: writes out first sketch of his theory of evolution (". . . my Species Theory.")

1846: begins his study of barnacles ("There is an extraordinary pleasure in pure observation.")

> *1847: Anesthesia with chloroform is discovered*

> *1848: The Communist Manifesto by Karl Marx and Friedrich Engels is published*

1848: Robert Darwin, Charles's father, dies ("My poor father died and no one who did not know him would believe that a man above eighty-three years could have retained so tender and affectionate a disposition.")

> *1849: California Gold Rush*

1856: begins his great book on evolution ("Early in 1856 Lyell advised me to write out my views pretty fully and I began at once to do so.")

1858: Atlantic cable is laid

1858: Wallace-Darwin paper on natural selection is read before the Linnean Society ("I was at first unwilling to consent as I thought Mr. Wallace might consider my doing so unjustifiable.")

1859, November 24: publication of *The Origin of Species* ("Well, good or bad, my work, Thank God, is over.")

1861-1865: American Civil War

1864: receives the Copley Medal of the Royal Society ("It shows that Natural Selection is making some progress in this country.")

1869: First transcontinental American railroad

1870: Franco-Prussian War; Third French Republic

1871: publication of *The Descent of Man* ("Everyone is talking about it without being shocked.")

1876: Alexander Graham Bell invents the telephone

1879: Thomas A. Edison invents the electric light bulb

1882: Triple Alliance of Germany, Austria, and Italy

1882, April 19: Charles Darwin dies.

Index